continuing professional development in education

C000018077

Challenging Behaviour – Understanding and Responding

A teacher's guide from Primary to Secondary

Paul Hamill

Series editor: Brian Boyd
Published in association with the
Times Educational Supplement Scotland

HODDER
GIBSON
PART OF HACHETTE LIVRE UK

Every effort has been made to trace all copyright holders, but if any have been inadvertently overlooked the Publishers will be pleased to make the necessary arrangements at the first opportunity.

Although every effort has been made to ensure that website addresses are correct at time of going to press, Hodder Gibson cannot be held responsible for the content of any website mentioned in this book. It is sometimes possible to find a relocated web page by typing in the address of the home page for a website in the URL window of your browser.

Hachette's policy is to use papers that are natural, renewable and recyclable products and made from wood grown in sustainable forests. The logging and manufacturing processes are expected to conform to the environmental regulations of the country of origin.

Orders: please contact Bookpoint Ltd, 130 Milton Park, Abingdon, Oxon OX14 4SB. Telephone: (44) 01235 827720. Fax: (44) 01235 400454. Lines are open 9.00–5.00, Monday to Saturday, with a 24-hour message answering service. Visit our website at www.hoddereducation.co.uk. Hodder Gibson can be contacted direct on: Tel: 0141 848 1609; Fax: 0141 889 6315; email: hoddergibson@hodder.co.uk

© Paul Hamill 2008

First published in 2008 by

Hodder Gibson, an imprint of Hodder Education, part of Hachette Livre UK, 2a Christie Street Paisley PA1 1NB

ISBN-13: 978 0340 947 821

Impression number   5 4 3 2 1
Year   2012 2011 2010 2009 2008

All rights reserved. Apart from any use permitted under UK copyright law, no part of this publication may be reproduced or transmitted in any form or by any means, electronic or mechanical, including photocopying and recording, or held within any information storage and retrieval system, without permission in writing from the publisher or under licence from the Copyright Licensing Agency Limited. Further details of such licences (for reprographic reproduction) may be obtained from the Copyright Licensing Agency Limited, Saffron House, 6–10 Kirby Street, London EC1N 8TS.

Cover illustration by David Parkin

Typeset by Transet Ltd, Coventry, England.

Printed in Great Britian by CPI Antony Rowe.

A catalogue record for this title is available from the British Library.

About the Author

Paul Hamill has worked in the field of education for nearly forty years and is a Senior Lecturer in the Department of Educational and Professional Studies at the University of Strathclyde. He was the Head of the Department of Educational Support and Guidance at the University for twelve years and taught for eighteen years in Primary, Secondary and Special schools.

He specialises in 'additional support needs' and his main research interests relate to the needs of children and young people who experience social, emotional and behavioural difficulties. He also studies the broad range of issues surrounding inclusion and inclusive education.

Paul is widely recognised as an educational consultant and, in particular, for the CPD opportunities he plans and delivers to local authorities, schools, teachers and other professionals. As a grandfather he continues to be aware of the significant impact effective teachers have on the lives of children and young people and his role as a teacher-educator remains his top priority.

Paul can be contacted at p.hamill@strath.ac.uk

Acknowledgements

This book is dedicated with love to my wife Sheila – an inspirational teacher.

Foreword

The *Times Educational Supplement Scotland* is delighted to be associated with the publication of another book in the Hodder Gibson series dedicated to key areas in the field of continuing professional development.

Since the newspaper's birth in 1965, we have always attempted to inform, educate and, occasionally, entertain the Scottish teaching profession, as well as to encourage dialogue between all educational sectors. In recent years, our commitment to the concept of encouraging educationists constantly to reflect – and act – upon best practice has been most tangibly evident in the special feature on CPD which we run twice a year.

This series of books offers a more permanent testimony of our commitment to CPD. Drawing on the experience of foremost Scottish practitioners, each book attempts to offer academic rigour with a lightness of delivery that is too often found wanting in the weightier tomes that populate many educational libraries, and which are consequently left unread, except by those approaching examinations – or job interviews.

Although we hope these books will be welcomed in the 'groves of academe', we also believe they deserve to be read – and acted upon – by a much wider audience: those teachers across Scotland in the nursery, primary and secondary sectors who deliver the curriculum on a daily basis to our young people.

Neil Munro
Editor, *Times Educational Supplement Scotland*

Contents

Challenging behaviour – a complex concept

> ❛ They will lie or thieve, swindle and deceive without cause or reason and punishment avails nothing to correct their extraordinary conduct. ❜
>
> **(Laurie, 1912)**

Introduction

The presumption of mainstreaming is now firmly enshrined in Scottish law. This means that as we move into the twenty-first century, our education system is now deeply rooted in the guiding principle that all young people have a right to be educated in their local mainstream school. The Standards in Scotland's Schools Etc. Act 2000 puts inclusion at the heart of our education system and rejects much traditional practice as discriminatory, based on outdated child deficit models which promoted segregation and exclusion for some young people.

The Education (Additional Support for Learning) (Scotland) Act 2004 takes this theme forward by moving the concept of additional support needs from the periphery to the centre of an effective education system. However, this Act still acknowledges that for some young people, inclusion in mainstream schools may not be in their best interests. For these individuals inclusion is about placing them in the environment which best meets their needs and this could include provision outwith mainstream or in support units within mainstream.

One group of young people who pose particular challenges within the mainstream sector are those whose behaviour is deemed to be so challenging that it is acting as a barrier to their learning and to the learning of their peers. The report *Count Us In – Achieving Inclusion in Scottish Schools* (HMIE, 2002) identified these young people as presenting particular challenges to schools. There is ample research evidence to suggest that when the concept of inclusion focuses upon young people whose behaviour can be disruptive the issues become much more complex and highly charged (Cooper, 1993; O'Brien, 1998; Hamill and Boyd, 2003; Porter, 2007).

These young people are often described as having social, emotional and behavioural difficulties (SEBD) and all too often become alienated and marginalised, resulting in the rejection of the school culture, which they perceive as devaluing them, and thus they become disaffected.

It is not easy for teachers to meet the needs of these young people whose difficult behaviour often masks their deep unhappiness and vulnerability. However, most teachers want to do their best for them and constantly seek answers in relation to how best to work with and support them.

Challenging behaviour – a new phenomenon?

One basic question which is often asked is the extent to which challenging behaviour has increased in recent years. This is a difficult question to answer and it is one which will be raised again elsewhere in this book. Schools, however, are not islands – they are set within the context of society as a whole and consequently they reflect the values of that society. Social change has been quite dramatic over the past few years and, in particular, the focus upon human rights and social inclusion has resulted in more young people whose behaviour can be disruptive being included in mainstream schools. It seems logical to suggest, therefore, that the number of young people whose behaviour gives cause for concern may not actually have increased but there are now many more young people included in mainstream schools who in the past would have been educated in some other form of external provision.

The current emphasis is placed upon the development of an educational system which is flexible enough to cater for a wide range of diversity. This includes young people whose behaviour is troubling and this poses particular challenges for schools. Over the past few years a radical change in thinking has occurred in relation to how we perceive the needs of young people.

This change has taken place within a social and cultural context which has shaped thinking and established the foundations upon which policy has developed and been translated into practice. To get a real grasp of this process, it is vital to understand fully the historical context which has influenced and impacted upon the present view of what constitutes good practice in relation to meeting the needs of young people whose behaviour is disruptive. Two important questions must be addressed at the outset:

1   How has the concept of social, emotional and behavioural difficulties (SEBD) evolved?
2   How has this shaped our perceptions of young people and their needs?

Before doing so, however, it is worthwhile to briefly consider the extent to which disruptive behaviour is a new phenomenon. Furlong (1985) considered what he referred to as deviant behaviour from a range of sociological perspectives and concluded that the history of disruptive behaviour can be traced from the inception of mass education itself. Ford *et al.* (1982) also make the case that policy makers faced a dilemma after state education became compulsory in 1870. It became clear at that time that there were young people in the education system whose behaviour was such that they were in need of social control. It was assumed that this group of young people would come mainly from the lower classes, and that they would have to be segregated, as their presence in school would have a negative impact upon their peers. It was important to find a solution to what was perceived to be a complex problem. The answer came in the form of categorisation and segregation, based initially on a medical model, and a psychological response to what was considered to be deviant behaviour: exclusion from the mainstream state schools.

Morally defective, maladjusted, deviant – a deficit model

To understand fully where we are at present in relation to policy and provision for young people with SEBD it is very important that we take an historical perspective which helps us to set the context in which traditional attitudes and expectations have evolved. In 1912, Laurie outlined in *The Teachers' Encyclopaedia* the philosophy which was to underpin professional thinking for most of the twentieth century. Young people whose behaviour did not conform to the accepted norm were considered to be 'affected by moral abnormalities' (p. 224). Challenging or disruptive behaviour was viewed in terms of a medical model and young people were diagnosed and labelled as morally defective. Thus behavioural difficulties were regarded as an illness which had to be treated and this often involved placing young people in residential institutions in rural surroundings were they could be removed from what were perceived to be 'the evil influences of bad homes and squalid streets' (p. 225).

In some cases the moral defect was considered to be organic and for these young people the outlook was thought to be hopeless. Longer-term detention was the answer as society had to be protected from their anti-social instincts. Education was seen not as a right but as having the potential to increase their powers of mischief.

In 1913 the Mental Deficiency Act identified the category of 'moral imbecile' or 'defective'. This negative label also covered those young people who are currently referred to as displaying disruptive behaviour as a result of social, emotional and behavioural difficulties. Provision for these individuals was firmly underpinned by a medical model which emphasised the need for segregation and social control. The young person was the problem and the response was psychological. They did not fit the system and required the help of doctors or the growing profession of psychology to help cure their abnormal behaviour.

The 1944 Education Act introduced the category of the 'maladjusted child' and in 1945 the Handicapped Pupils and School Health Regulations officially defined some young people as maladjusted and placed them in the 'handicapped' category. The term 'maladjusted' was largely used as an umbrella term and included a range of factors implying inherent individual deficiencies, personal inadequacies and moral deviance. This reinforced the message conveyed by the eugenics movement which, at this time, viewed the behaviour of disruptive individuals as a direct result of their social class. These young people were assumed to belong mainly to the lower class and were a product of the deficiencies associated with it. Galloway *et al.* (1994) sum up this concept of maladjustment very effectively when they state that:

> the social identity of any child assessed post 1944 as maladjusted and later as emotionally and behaviourally disturbed, is one which has a powerful history of stigma, being associated with undesirable personal and social circumstances.
>
> (p. 112)

The process of categorisation was reinforced in Scotland in 1954 by the Special Education Treatment (Scotland) Regulations. This system was described by Ainscow (1991, p. 2) as 'a process of labelling which encouraged the creation of stereotypes that disadvantaged those involved'.

The *Underwood Report* of the Committee on Maladjusted Children (MoE, 1955) marked a significant landmark in relation to the development of ideas surrounding the concept of maladjustment and the treatment of the disorder. The focus was placed upon the classification of symptoms such as nervous disorders, habit disorders, organic disorders and psychotic disorders. Thus the reference to symptoms and the allusion to psychiatrists clearly reflected the prevailing attitudes to young people who experienced social, emotional and behavioural difficulties. The medical model dominated professional thinking and set the context for practice by considering the source of all behavioural difficulties to reside within the individuals themselves.

It is clear that the term 'maladjusted' evolved in a context where it was embedded in a deficit philosophy that linked it to a prevailing medical model which emphasised the concept of mental deficiency. Galloway *et al.* (1994) make the point very effectively when they talk about children who display emotionally disturbed behaviour as being synonymous with those considered to be moral imbeciles or moral defectives (1913 Mental Deficiency Act). The label 'maladjustment' was always difficult to define and Laslett (1983) describes it as a catch-all for children who display a wide range of both learning and/or behavioural difficulties.

In the 1960s, maladjusted behaviour was often equated with deviance and abnormality (Becker, 1963; Ullman and Krasner, 1965). Young people were often described as disturbed because their behaviour was not seen to be consistent with accepted cultural norms. Concepts such as 'morally defective', 'deviant' and 'maladjusted' received high priority throughout most of the twentieth century; a change in attitudes and a rethinking of this deficit philosophy did not occur until the late 1970s.

Extending our vision

In the latter part of the twentieth century there was a move towards social change which promoted equal opportunity and a commitment to inclusion. The label 'maladjusted' became recognised as vague and imprecise, and gradually young people came to be viewed in terms of their individual needs as opposed to their perceived inbuilt deficiencies.

The Warnock Report, published in 1978 (DES), became an important landmark in relation to these changes. The report emphasised the concept of need as opposed to handicap and reflected 'both the gradual disenchantment with statutory categories and the developing rhetoric of integration' (Gilbert and Hart, 1990, p. 18). It introduced the concept of special educational need in place of the traditional process of categorisation of handicaps and deficiencies and also had an impact on young people who had previously been labelled as maladjusted.

This latter group were recognised as having social, emotional and behavioural difficulties, thus providing a more precise description of young people whose behaviour gives cause for concern. This was, of course, a step in the right direction but although the new label 'social, emotional and behavioural difficulties' had more positive connotations, it still focused largely upon perceived deficits inherent within the individual. This meant that, in reality, these young people were still seen as a group set apart from other learners and accepted as having special educational needs due to their physical, sensory, and learning difficulties. The concept of special educational needs gradually emerged in the late 1970s and the basic rationale which shaped this process was the move away from focusing upon inbuilt deficiencies to the recognition that special needs can arise from inappropriate systems, particularly from an inaccessible curriculum. Teachers were encouraged to rethink their educational philosophies and move away from restricted definitions which tended to place the source of a young person's learning or behavioural difficulty outwith the school. However, there still remained a strong tendency to view young people whose behaviour was disruptive as being entirely responsible for that behaviour. They were seen to be choosing to misbehave and able to control this behaviour if they so wished.

In 1999, *A Manual of Good Practice in Special Educational Needs* (SOEID) endorsed the view outlined in 1994 in the *Effective Provision for Special Educational Needs* report (SOED, p. 7) which identified the concept of special educational needs as one which is 'subtle and requires discussion and reflection'. It acknowledged that it was not easy to provide a working definition of the concept of special educational needs, as a range of needs had to be accounted for within such a definition. The needs of young people who experienced social, emotional and behavioural difficulties were now included within this more diverse, wide-ranging definition. Special needs were now seen to arise from: 'social factors within the home or school, which affect the individual's capacity to learn and from delays or disturbances in emotional development' (SOED, 1994, p. 8)

Gradually a more enlightened philosophy emerged which emphasised the need for all professionals to internalise a shared understanding of the concept of special educational needs. This understanding was seen to be vital if effective planning and provision for a range of needs were to be put in place at all levels of the education system. The overarching principle which now informed thinking was that special educational needs arise from barriers to learning and these barriers were now recognised as being more complex and diverse.

It is, of course, very important to appreciate fully what is meant by 'difficulty in learning'. It must be viewed from a fairly wide perspective to include not only cognitive ability but also the affective dimension. Young people whose behaviour can be disruptive often have difficulty developing social competence, adjusting to social contexts and learning to follow normal and accepted patterns of behaviour.

Having said all of this, it remains necessary to clarify further what is meant by the term 'social, emotional and behavioural difficulties' and once again it becomes clear that arriving at a definition is not an easy matter.

Defining social, emotional and behavioural difficulties

Young people whose behaviour is problematic can pose a challenge in school, at home and in the community. This is summed up in the report by HM Inspectorate of Education *Count Us In – Achieving Inclusion in Scottish Schools* which states that 'major challenges are presented... by the need to address better the needs of pupils who are alienated or disaffected from school' (HMIE, 2002, p. 4).

Meeting the needs of these young people can be a complex business and involves a wide range of professionals including teachers, educational psychologists, social workers, community education workers and, in some cases, the police. If these needs are not met effectively, all too often the result is underachievement, disaffection and exclusion from school. We must take great care when we attempt to define the characteristics of this group. Labelling individuals as SEBD is in itself a concern as it can set them apart from others who have additional support needs.

In 1993 some of the common characteristics of this particular group were presented in Part 3 Section 6 of the report entitled *Support for Learning: Special Educational Needs Within the 5–14 Curriculum* (SCCC, 1993) as follows:

- low self-esteem
- lack of motivation
- lack of concentration
- difficulties in learning
- poor interpersonal skills
- feelings of helplessness.

Young people who experience social, emotional and behavioural difficulties inevitably face barriers which adversely affect the learning process. It can be difficult to pinpoint the exact nature of these barriers as they often emerge as a result of a number of interrelated factors. Cooper (1993, p. 9) suggests that to understand problematic behaviour we must take into account the 'complex interaction between contextual factors and aspects which the individual brings to the situation'.

Research evidence (Hamill and Boyd, 2003) continues to support the view that the deficit model still prevails in many schools where young people who display challenging behaviour are all too often perceived in terms of the problems they pose to their teachers and their peers. Many educationalists have emphasised the need to avoid this exclusive focus on a deficit philosophy (Garner and Gains, 1996; Montgomery, 1998; O'Brien, 1998). They argue that an overemphasis on this model results in little attention being paid to the wider ranging sources of behavioural difficulties which are, in fact, outwith the control of the young person.

Although it is very important to question the adherence to the deficit model, it is also necessary to recognise that some disruptive behaviour may result from fairly serious, often deep-rooted, psychological problems (Farrell, 1995). This generally includes a minority of young people, but it should be kept in mind that some young people may suffer from psychiatric conditions, or genetic or biological difficulties (Cole *et al.*, 1998).

Thus the term 'social, emotional and behavioural difficulties' can be applied to a fairly wide range of young people: from those who misbehave sporadically and for a relatively short stage in their development to those whose behaviour can be extremely challenging and who, in some cases, may display deep-rooted and long-term psycho-social difficulties. Many of these young people pose problems for their schools and often the only solution is seen to be exclusion. Barber (1996, p. 20) refers to these excluded young people as 'the disadvantaged, the disaffected and the disappeared'. He alludes to a vicious circle which begins with underachievement fuelling disaffection and exclusion leading to detachment from the education system. Social, emotional and behavioural difficulties manifest themselves in different ways depending on the young person. Some young people are explosive and volatile, aggressive and sometimes violent, while others are isolated, withdrawn and introverted. As previously indicated, defining this group is not easy. It is very clear that many of the difficulties experienced have their source rooted deeply in early childhood and that the impact of the schooling process also plays a significant part in determining behaviour. It is important therefore to consider the influence of the home and school in relation to shaping behaviour.

The impact of home and school

Home

Problematic behaviour such as aggression, attention seeking and social detachment often has its source in childhood, and results from inappropriate physical and emotional nurturing in the early years. When this occurs, children do not have access to appropriate role models and therefore they lack the opportunity to learn appropriate behavioural responses. It is now universally acknowledged that the role parents play in relation to their child's education is very important and this role is nowhere more crucial than in relation to those who have additional support needs and, in particular, those with social, emotional and behavioural needs. Research evidence (Reid, 1987; Herbert, 1993; Evans *et al.*, 1999) consistently supports the view that children who are seriously disaffected and whose behaviour gives cause for concern often come from socially and economically disadvantaged families. Cooper (1993) summarises this evidence and suggests that young people in these circumstances are likely to have experienced:

- lack of parental interest in schooling
- inconsistent and ineffectual parental discipline
- parental indifference, hostility, aggression and rejection
- parental cruelty/neglect and parental absences
- violent/aggressive parents.

It is, of course, all too easy to put the blame on parents and one must be extremely careful not to simply equate behavioural difficulties with ineffective parenting. In reality the situation is often much more complex. In 1999, the Scottish Council Foundation illustrated this complexity when it said that 'a society in which having children is a participatory factor for poverty and disadvantage alongside long-term illness and unemployment is not one that supports and values children and parenting' (SCF, 1999, p. 28).

Some parents have themselves experienced problems in their own childhood and have to cope on a daily basis with extremely demanding lives, which often makes it difficult for them to provide the quality of care and support their children need and deserve. Many parents try in difficult circumstances to do their best, but there is little doubt that a sizeable number of young people live in environments which are physically, socially and emotionally impoverished. The culture of the community in which they live may not support the norms and patterns of behaviour expected in school. Academic achievement may in fact be given a fairly low priority in communities whose value system differs markedly from that which underpins the schooling process.

In these circumstances, parents can come to be perceived as indifferent, uncaring and unwilling to co-operate with the school. We must take great care that we do not simply allow these negative parental stereotypes to go unchallenged or they will present barriers to home–school partnerships which will be very difficult to break down. This places an additional burden on schools who must constantly strive to reach out to these parents who themselves may be disaffected and who do not fully appreciate the value of education.

School

There is now an increasing body of evidence which indicates that a young person's experience at school also plays an important part in shaping behaviour. Schools and teachers can both reduce and produce disaffection (Reynolds and Sullivan, 1981; Booth and Coulby, 1987; Fogell and Long, 1997; Montgomery, 1998). One influential report which focused on the impact schools have on the behaviour of their pupils confirmed that a number of significant school factors were particularly relevant. This report, entitled *Education for Disaffected Pupils* (DES, 1993), surveyed pupils in 31 primary schools and 18 secondary schools in England and identified the following features as being associated with the promotion of positive behaviour:

- the curriculum was generally matched to the pupil's needs, aptitudes and abilities
- most teachers enjoyed the company of their pupils and expressed interest in them
- classrooms were orderly places
- a wide range of formal and informal awards were used and applied consistently by the majority of staff
- lessons were well prepared and clearly delivered using a range of appropriate teaching styles
- sanctions were fair and understood by pupils and parents. They were seen to be appropriate to the offence and applied flexibly and consistently
- the marking of pupils' work was constructive with regular feedback on quality of presentation and attainment.

In 1979, Rutter *et al.* demonstrated clearly that schools make a difference and they can provide environments where positive behaviour is enhanced and promoted or where negative behaviours thrive in a context of disaffection. One important way that schools can make a difference is through the curriculum, which can either produce or reduce disaffection. The curriculum is a powerful tool which, when effectively planned and developed, can be used to enhance behaviour. Where it is inappropriate and inaccessible it can be a major source of difficulty for some young people who see it as irrelevant to their lives. It is sometimes painful to appreciate and accept that some young people may not learn effectively and may behave badly because of how and what they are taught.

It would appear, therefore, that schools do have some control over a range of factors which affect behaviour and teachers can play a significant role in alleviating or exacerbating difficult behaviour. As is the case with parents, the focus must never be on apportioning blame but upon recognising what schools and teachers do effectively and ensuring this becomes the norm.

There can be no doubt that the teacher's job can be difficult, especially when young people are demotivated and disinterested. In such circumstances the teacher can feel devalued and demoralised, and it is all too easy for a vicious circle to emerge where teachers become reluctant to continually give their best to young people who do not appear to respond. However, the majority of teachers are professionals who do all in their power to provide a quality education for young people. There are however, teachers who are less effective in their ability to reflect upon and analyse their own practice as a contributing factor to the behavioural difficulties displayed by some young people. It has to be acknowledged that some teachers become disaffected and, regardless of the reasons for this, it seems obvious that when the disaffected pupil encounters the disaffected teacher, the stage is set for inevitable disruption, stress and the breakdown of the teacher–pupil relationship.

It would therefore be extremely difficult to dispute the view that schools make a difference and that they can provide environments where positive behaviour is enhanced and promoted or where negative behaviour can thrive in a context of disaffection.

Behavioural difficulties – an additional support need

In 2003 the SEED report *Moving Forward! Additional Support for Learning* proposed a new legislative framework which replaced the label 'special educational needs' with one which was seen to be more positive – 'additional support needs'. This terminology was perceived to be less likely to stigmatise and negatively categorise young people. One group of young people who were clearly recognised as having additional needs were those experiencing social, emotional and behavioural difficulties. Thus as we entered the new millennium this group of young people were included among those who required additional support.

Nonetheless there is evidence to suggest that many teachers still do not consider young people who present challenging behaviour as a result of experiencing social, emotional and behavioural difficulties to have additional support needs. Hamill and Boyd (2003) surveyed over 2000 secondary and primary teachers in relation to their experiences of working with young people whose behaviour could be challenging. When asked if these young people had special educational/additional support needs the majority of teachers felt that these young people did not have additional support needs but were in fact making a conscious choice to be difficult. Many teachers adopted a deficit philosophy and located the source of behavioural difficulties within the young person.

This view does not resonate with current thinking, as can be seen from the Education (Additional Support for Learning) (Scotland) Act 2004. Professionals are now encouraged to cast their net more widely when thinking about the barriers to learning faced by some young people. It is now recognised that a diverse range of circumstances may give rise to additional support needs and several of these circumstances relate clearly to the area of behaviour:

- children with Attention Deficit/Hyperactivity Disorder (AD/HD)
- children who are bullying or being bullied
- children who live in violent environments
- children/young people who are in conflict with the law because of offending behaviour
- children whose educational development is suffering (including those who are excluded).

The *Supporting Children's Learning: Code of Practice* (SE, 2005) emphasised that a wide range of factors may lead to some young people having a need for additional support. These include social and emotional factors and it is made clear that 'a child with behavioural difficulties may require additional support to develop positive behaviour in school and to stop offending in the community' (SE, 2005, p. 20).

It remains to be seen if this *Code of Practice* will make a significant difference to the quality of support young people receive. In particular it will be interesting to see what impact it has in schools in relation to including those whose behaviour gives cause for concern. Creating codes of practice like this is one thing but ensuring that teachers and other professionals have internalised the attitudes and expectations which will be vital to the success of it is quite a different matter.

SUMMARY

One of the major issues facing schools today is how they can effectively support and include young people whose behaviour can be challenging. Effective teachers strive to develop skills in managing inappropriate behaviour but realise there are no quick fixes or easy solutions. Before we can manage disruptive behaviour which arises from social, emotional and behavioural difficulties it is vitally important that we understand that such a concept is multifaceted and complex.

Traditionally, the young people who experienced behavioural difficulties were viewed in terms of what was perceived to be their inbuilt deficiencies. Labels such as 'maladjusted', 'deviant' and 'morally defective' summed up the adherence to this deficit philosophy which held sway for much of the twentieth century.

In the latter part of that century thinking began to change and it was recognised that the source of much of the behaviour displayed by these young people was to some extent outwith their control. The impact of home and school factors began to be seriously considered and this provided food for thought and encouraged professionals to rethink attitudes and expectations rooted within a deficit model.

As we move into the twenty-first century, it is now accepted that some young people have additional support needs which are covered by the emerging legislation. In particular the *Code of Practice* (2005) outlines what will constitute effective practice in supporting children's learning, and it is within this context that the needs of those whose behaviour impairs their ability to benefit fully from the educational experiences must be considered.

POINTS FOR REFLECTION

1 Do teachers and other professionals understand what is meant by the term 'social, emotional and behavioural difficulties (SEBD)'? Do they see it as a multifaceted concept or do they still use a deficit model to shape their understanding?

2 Some young people become alienated and marginalised as a result of their experiences at school. Why does this happen? Research suggests that effective schools and teachers can play a significant part in reducing disaffection. Do you agree?

3 What is meant by the term 'additional support needs'? Should young people who, as a result of social, emotional and behavioural difficulties, display challenging behaviour be seen to have additional support needs?

2 Understanding challenging behaviour

> The fact that there are different and conflicting theories explaining maladjustment in children is not of enormous importance to teachers. What is important is their appreciation of what each approach has to offer and the effectiveness of the one they choose.

(Laslett, 1977)

Simple solutions and quick fixes

It is clear that schools have to demonstrate that they are catering for, responding appropriately to, and effectively supporting the increasingly diverse needs of young people who are educated within them. There can be little doubt that one group of young people who present particular challenges to teachers and other professionals who support them are those whose behaviour is disruptive.

In December 2000 the Minister for Education established a Discipline Task Group (DTG) to examine the issue of indiscipline in Scottish schools. It was acknowledged that the majority of teachers felt that the process of learning and teaching was being adversely affected by an increase in unacceptable behaviour which disrupted the education of these young people themselves and their non-disruptive peers. The DTG's response to concerns expressed over indiscipline was conveyed in the report *Better Behaviour – Better Learning* (BBBL) (SEED, 2001).

This report concurred with much of the recent research in relation to challenging behaviour, emphasising that it was a complex, multidimensional concept. There was a strong focus placed upon the nature and range of social factors which impact on the lives of young people most likely to have social, emotional and behavioural difficulties. The BBBL report included the following factors:

- poor basic skills
- poor relationships with other pupils/parents/carers or teachers
- pressure from others to behave in a way which may conflict with authority
- parents or carers unable to exercise control
- exposure to physical or sexual abuse
- victims of racism.

(SEED, 2001, p. 12)

There is no doubt that young people whose behaviour is challenging can disrupt the whole process of teaching and learning. They drain the energy of even the most effective teachers and play their part in raising teachers' stress levels. However, these young people are not always easy to understand and getting to grips with what makes them tick involves an acceptance that they are often fairly complex individuals with fairly deep-rooted problems. Their challenging behaviour can be displayed in a myriad of ways such as anxiety, depression, apathy, isolation, aggression, self-harm, attention-seeking, vulnerability, rejection and violence. There is no set mould into which all of these young people can be fitted; even within this group there is considerable diversity.

There is no doubt that even in these circumstances many teachers provide excellent support for these young people and, from my own experience of providing continuing professional development to teachers across Scotland, many continue to look for feasible solutions. It would be wrong to say that there are no answers, but it would be fair to say that there are no quick fixes or easy solutions. Finding answers requires the teacher to ask the right questions and this can involve critical scrutiny of practice, professional reflection and a genuine attempt to understand why some young people behave as they do. Teachers constantly strive to find strategies that will improve behaviour but it is important to see that strategies operate at two levels.

Level 1 – At this foundation level teachers have to give careful consideration to the extent to which they have internalised the philosophy which underpins the nature and range of challenging behaviours. First and foremost they must be able to stand back and take time to explore their understanding of some of the root causes of disruptive behaviour. They will then be more receptive to the behaviour management strategies which are presented at level two.

Level 2 – This level develops and extends the knowledge gained through personal and professional reflection at level one. The main focus is to use this knowledge to enhance practice in the classroom by implementing effective positive behaviour management strategies in a flexible manner taking full account of the young person's needs.

This chapter explores some of the important issues relating to level one above. The more practical strategies relating to level two will be addressed in later chapters.

Why do some young people behave badly?

Over the past few years, innumerable books have been produced to help teachers develop effective behaviour management strategies (McSherry, 2001; Glenn et al., 2004; Rogers, 2004; Leaman, 2005; Farrell, 2006). These publications present ideas to teachers in relation to how they might promote more positive behaviour and consequently create environments which are more conducive to learning. Strategies are not always easy to implement but many effective teachers strive to put them into practice in their classrooms and do so successfully. There are also teachers who respond by asserting that these behaviour management strategies do not work and who are not prepared to examine in any real depth why this might be the case. This is not about apportioning blame to teachers, and there are, of course, a range of reasons why some strategies do not work. Teachers, however, who find it difficult to implement strategies must not be allowed to simply assert that the strategies don't work. Many of these behaviour management strategies do have a positive impact on behaviour and they do work but only in the hands of a reflective professional who is able to put their practice under the microscope and see that their attitudes and expectations may be the stumbling block. Teachers cannot force pupils to behave but they can shape appropriate behaviour and encourage pupils to take the responsibility to change their own behaviour. Effective behaviour management involves adapting and modifying strategies to fit the individual pupil and the classroom situation. It does not involve using approaches which exert control over behaviour nor the adherence to a set of rigid strategies applied uniformly in an authoritarian manner. Catering for diversity implies the ability to make the strategies fit the individual. It is, however, vital that we start by emphasising that the first strategy a teacher must internalise is an understanding of why some young people behave badly. This understanding provides the fundamental cornerstone on which we build good practice. Without it, teachers will find it very difficult to appreciate behaviour as a multifaceted complex phenomenon. There is no easy route to understanding why some young people display disturbed or disruptive behaviour. The needs of this group lie on a broad spectrum from those who occasionally misbehave and whose difficulties are relatively short term to those who are extremely challenging or have serious psychological difficulties. Effective practice in relation to supporting young people (SEBD) will depend on an understanding of the behavioural theories which provide some explanation as to the sources of this challenging behaviour.

Psychodynamic theory

This theory is based upon the work of Sigmund Freud who encouraged a psycho-therapeutic approach whereby individuals are encouraged to explore the inner world of emotions and the route through which these emotions are developed.

Emphasis is placed upon early childhood development and the nature, range and quality of infantile experiences. Deprivation in the early years of a child's life is seen to be a fundamental barrier to healthy emotional development and high importance is placed upon the fact that when young people display difficult behaviour it can often be traced to trauma in early childhood. This is summed up by Cooper (2004) when he discusses how unsatisfactory early childhood relationships with primary carers can lead to feelings of alienation and insecurity. This reinforces the work done by individuals such as Bowlby (1971) who demonstrated how attachment difficulties can adversely effect the child's development; Laslett (1977) who emphasised the basic needs of a small child as love, safety and esteem; and Winnicott (1991) who made the causal link between disturbed parenting and the emotional damage it can inflict on the child.

This damage is often done in the early stages of a child's development when the significant adults in their lives cannot or will not provide the emotional support which comes from the provision of unconditional love. Unfortunately it is all too often the case that these adults are themselves victims of the very circumstances their children now find themselves in. Individuals become trapped in a vicious circle and it is very difficult to break out. Some parents have poorly developed parenting skills and although it may be done unconsciously, they play their part in the continuation of a self-fulfilling prophecy which sees problem behaviour as an inevitable part of life. The following scenario provides some insight into how this damaging process operates.

Scenario 1

Paul is a four year old boy who has been excluded from the nursery on three occasions because of his aggressive behaviour. On the last occasion he punched a little girl in the eye and when the teacher tried to intervene he pushed her and swore at her. At home he lives with his mum and her latest partner and they both try to do what they perceive as their best for Paul. They often resort to physical punishment and say as it was good enough for them it is good enough for Paul. The parents were told at the last nursery parent's night that they should try to play with Paul. They tried it and it seemed to work but they gave up because they could not sustain the effort involved. Paul constantly hears loud aggressive language and swearing; sometimes his parents' arguments become a bit too physical. Paul's mum has a very poor relationship with her own father whom she never sees. When she does speak of him, she says he was a bully who never cared what happened to her. Paul is a desperately unhappy little boy and he got very upset recently when he heard his mum say to her partner that she thinks Paul is just a bad boy and she finds it hard to love him. She told Paul he would go to prison one day like his real dad if his behaviour does not improve. Paul reacted by ripping the wallpaper off the living room wall and kicking the dog. His step-dad put him into his bedroom and told him he was to stay there until he had calmed down.

Meeting the needs of young children is not only a biological process, it is also an emotional one. When this process is interactive and takes place within a loving relationship it enables strong emotional bonds to be forged. Continuity of experience is vital to the child and when this collapses the result can be emotional impairment. This impairment can remain with an individual throughout life and manifest itself in behavioural difficulties. It is not easy to rectify the effects of emotional deprivation in infancy and as young people grow up, their challenging behaviour can actually be seen as an attempt to reclaim what was not forthcoming in infancy. A range of difficult behaviour may ensue. The following classification of common behaviours provides a useful frame of reference.

Psychodynamic theory	
Conduct disorders	**Neurotic disorders**
Anti-social aggressive behaviour. Unable to settle, attention seeking. Irrational, angry and hostile. Tendency to be extra-punitive, blaming problems on other children, adults and/or the outside world. Rebels against and questions authority. Needs to be the centre of attention but challenging behaviour often masks an underlying vulnerability.	Withdrawn isolated behaviour. Daydreaming, anxious and worried. Poor self-image and low self-esteem. Tendency to be intra-punitive blaming problems on themselves. Hides difficulties, sensitive and easily embarrassed. Often co-operative with those in authority and would prefer to avoid people.

Supporting these young people can be very difficult and time consuming. Effective intervention can be complex and requires professionals to be skilled in their ability to form trusting relationships with troubled individuals. Many of these young people require therapeutic approaches and counselling. In some cases this is on offer, but all too often these children are in mainstream classrooms and are not receiving this one-to-one support. In these circumstances many teachers are struggling to do their best, but realise that for these young people this is not good enough. I have argued here that the first crucial step is understanding where the bad behaviour comes from. This in itself is vital and can make a difference to the way teachers perceive these young people. However, the fact remains that few teachers receive adequate training in relation to the complexities of psychodynamic theory or the damage that can be done in early childhood.

Social learning theory

The development of this theory was heavily influenced by the work of Mischel (1973) and Bandura (1977) and the basic principle underpinning it is that behaviour occurs in specific situations and the forces which shape it lie within these situations. In essence this is a process whereby individuals learn to behave in particular ways and are strongly influenced by imitating the significant behavioural models presented to them as they develop emotionally. The most significant role models in the lives of children and young people are, of course, their parents or carers. Those who support this theory perceive these adults as representing a mirror reflecting particular behaviour, which is copied and internalised by the child, who takes it into all spheres of their life, including school.

The influence of role models is most powerful when behaviour is observed in situations which are highly charged emotionally. If a child's social and emotional development is left to parents who find it difficult to control their own feelings then children will be exposed to situations where verbal and/or physical aggression are the norm, and they may come to see such behaviour as acceptable and justifiable.

The following scenario gives an example of how this process operates in reality.

Scenario 2

A father comes home drunk after work. He is already angry and immediately takes this out on his partner. He shouts aggressively at her because she has not prepared his meal and he wants to go out with his friends. His anger explodes into violence and he punches her. She begins to cry and tries in vain to placate him.

The couple's two children (a boy and a girl) are present and observe the behaviour of both parents. The boy says nothing but once again resolves in his mind that when he grows up he will not resort to violent behaviour. In the same way the girl renews her determination not to be a future submissive victim. However, the power of these adult role models is very strong and it will be very difficult for the children not to internalise the observed behaviours. Some children will be resilient enough to do so, but some will struggle and may not be able to surmount the emotional barriers they face.

Social learning theory is built upon the belief that all behaviour is learned and can therefore also be unlearned. Individuals learn a range of typical behavioural responses and gradually build up a repertoire of these responses which they come to regard as acceptable, although in reality they are all too often totally inappropriate. The emphasis is placed upon the aspects of behaviour which can be measured through the process of observation. The overall focus is on the actual behaviour evident within a specific situation, as opposed to searching for the underlying causation, which might be deeply rooted in the subconscious mental processes.

Another central feature of this approach is the idea that behaviour which is reinforced will persist, and conversely, behaviour which is ignored will eventually diminish. Both desirable and undesirable behaviour can be reinforced. This can be done intentionally when adults who understand the complexity of behavioural development strive to model the behaviour they expect. Inappropriate behaviour can also be encouraged unintentionally when adults reinforce it by giving the child the attention they are seeking. The following scenario indicates how this can happen.

Scenario 3

A parent tends not to interact with her son. She does not play with him as often as she might because she sometimes feels a bit stressed as she has two younger children. At playgroup her son is a bit boisterous and when he wants a toy he takes it from children who are playing with it. This results in a tussle which the little boy usually wins. When this happens his mum intervenes, scolds him and insists that he returns the toy. He does so but this behaviour continues as her son has learned that this is how he gets her attention. She is in fact unintentionally reinforcing the unacceptable behaviour.

For some children whose behaviour is particularly demanding, their parents may give way over a particular point, and this can teach the child that the way to achieve their desired ends is to have a tantrum each time there is a dispute. Unfortunately many children learn that the attention of adults can often be more easily gained by displaying inappropriate behaviour than by displaying acceptable behaviour, even though they constantly receive the message from adults that they prefer the 'good' behaviour. Thus the disruptive behaviour comes to be more frequently reinforced than the satisfactory behaviour. These children come to school having experienced fairly ineffective role models. They therefore tend to be suspicious of all adults and have low expectations of them. For these children it is vital that their teachers are able to overcome these negative perceptions and to provide for them the positive role models which have so far been lacking in their lives. When this does not happen the young person's behavioural difficulties are compounded, but where the teacher realises that they are a very significant behavioural model in the lives of some children, then there is hope that the child's behaviour can change.

Systems theory

Systems theory highlights the fact that no man is an island and, therefore, a focus upon the individual as a way of understanding behaviour is a limited approach. Every human being exists within a wider group or system and is a vital part of these systems. A system can be characterised by its communication channels, its structure, the roles individuals play within it and the rules which enable it to function effectively. Porter (2007, p. 161) throws light on the concept of a system when she suggests that it implies that the fundamental indicator is that the group members 'interact in systematic ways that imply implicit rules and expectations'. There are observable patterns within the system which provide insight into the nature and range of relationships, and it is by examing these patterns that we can put in place a framework which can help us reflect upon recurring behavioural problems.

The basic premise which underpins this behavioural theory is that every individual lives within a set of interrelated subsystems. Bronfenbrenner (1979) studied the effect of ecosystems on human behaviour. He considered the impact of ecosystemic theory within the educational context presenting the following model to enhance the understanding of how a range of subsystems continually interact within a young person's life to produce particular forms of behaviour.

The microsystem	The individual child
The mesosystem	The individual child, his peers and his teacher(s)
The ecosystem	The individual child, the way he interacts at home, school, within the community and with other agencies
The macrosystem	The world as a whole and how the individual relates to the values, attitudes, expectations and beliefs portrayed in this global context

(Bronfenbrenner 1979)

This approach to behaviour was developed by Molnar and Lindquist (1989) who went further in considering its application to behaviour within the context of the school. The school is seen as a system interconnected to other systems such as the home, and the classroom is viewed as a sub-system within the school in particular, but also inextricably linked to the home. Proponents of ecosystemic theory emphasise that a change within any part of one system has an effect on the other systems. Behaviour must, therefore, be viewed within this holistic context if there is to be any real hope of sustained improvements. An example of how this process works is outlined in the following scenarios.

Scenario 4

A teenage boy's father is confined to prison and as a result the family lose their breadwinner. The mother has other fairly young children and she has to go out to work, relying increasingly on her son to act as a surrogate father to his siblings. He is missing school because she needs his support and he wants to do his best to help. He feels lost and vulnerable and this is affecting his schoolwork and behaviour. He feels that few of his teachers can empathise with him. His friends are not interested in his problems and he has no opportunity to express openly how he is feeling.

Scenario 5

A little girl aged ten is finding reading difficult. She is an intelligent girl who excels in practical subjects and until now she has been able to maintain her position in the middle attainment group in the class. She is well aware that there is a problem and she desperately wants it to go away. Her teacher has been doing what she can to provide additional support and some progress has been made. The teacher decides it would be best if she were extracted from class for additional reading support. The girl sees this as a negative step and she is very anxious and concerned that she will be seen as a failure. She is upset and she has started to refuse to go to school on the extraction days. Her parents don't know what to do and their daughter just clams up when they try to talk to her.

Dowling and Osborne (1994, p.3) provide some valuable insights into the systems approach to behaviour. They sum it up by saying that it provides 'a view of behaviour which takes account of the context in which it occurs' (p. 3). This means that an understanding of why some individuals behave badly can only be achieved by taking full account of all the contributing contextual factors. This involves adopting a holistic perspective rather than an individualistic perspective. Traditional thinking has tended to conceptualise behaviour as a linear concept and this has lead some professionals to explain behaviour in terms of the perceived causes, rather than by looking at the effects of the behaviour. Farrell (2006) sums this up by emphasising the need to focus on the 'how' as opposed to the 'why' question (p. 18). From this viewpoint it becomes much more productive to think about the process which shaped the behaviour, rather than spend time trying to analyse the resulting behaviour.

To view behaviour from a systems perspective, one needs to recognise the need to move away from viewing the locus of the problem behaviour within the individual, and to give much more significance to relationships. We must be wary of attempting to understand behaviour by trying to divide it up into its constituent parts. If we do so, the result may be that limited attention will be paid to the relationship between the behavioural elements. There is also a danger that we will underplay the importance of the quality of interaction. One particular advantage for teachers of taking a systemic perspective is that it enables them to extend their view away from simply looking at individual deficiencies, and encourages them to take a total overview when thinking about young people whose behaviour can be challenging.

Linking theory to practice

Professionals must consider all of these theories very carefully and they should be wary of accepting them uncritically. The theories are often complementary, and one theory alone may not necessarily provide the answer as to why some young people behave badly. It is vital to keep in mind that there are exceptions to every rule. For example, a young person may display complex aggressive acting-out behaviour while his siblings reared in the same environment by the same parents do not display these behaviours.

Some young people who are exposed to very negative role models are able to overcome the barriers they experience and go on to become well-adjusted individuals. Ultimately we must keep uppermost in our minds the fact that we are dealing with behaviour which is a complex phenomenon and which does not always conform to theoretical frameworks. However, it is still very worthwhile to consider the link between behavioural theories and the related interventionist approaches. I will look at this briefly from the perspective of all three theoretical models outlined in this chapter.

Psychodynamic theory

From this perspective the challenging behaviour displayed by some young people is rooted in their subconscious thoughts. Some of the most damaged and disturbed young people in our schools display their deviant behaviour by venting their anger and aggression in ways which are totally unacceptable. Many of their problems are linked to emotional deprivation in early childhood. In these cases some form of psychotherapy may be needed, aimed at helping the emotionally disturbed individual to change their behaviour in order to adjust more effectively to their environments.

Psychotherapeutic approaches aim to assist the troubled individual to disclose and hopefully deal with powerful unconscious feelings in a safe non-judgemental environment where they feel supported. This kind of therapeutic intervention provides the vital context in which individuals can start to recover emotionally. The focus is upon healing young people who have been emotionally damaged.

This group of young people comprise a sizeable minority in our schools, but there is evidence to suggest that increasing numbers may suffer from fairly serious psychological difficulties and mental health problems (Farrell, 1995). This situation was reinforced by Cole *et al.* (1998) when they indicated that some young people may suffer from fairly severe psychiatric conditions and may also experience genetic or biological abnormalities.

It is not difficult, therefore, to see why teachers often feel unprepared to take on the role of counsellor exploring the world of the young person whose emotional state is fragile. This must be acknowledged, and the teacher who has received no formal training in these areas must be very wary of releasing suppressed feelings when they do not have the specialist skills necessary to help the young person deal with them.

Schools and teachers must be vigilant at all times and seek the support these individuals require. They need to involve both psychological and health services where there are professionals who are equipped to provide the counselling and therapies needed. Accessing these services may be easier said than done as the demand usually well outweighs the resources available, and thus many young people who could benefit from these services are not given the opportunity to do so. They remain in schools where the vital therapeutic interventions do not materialise and where teachers strive to do their very best to meet their needs without the additional support they require.

It is obvious, therefore, that psychodynamic approaches take time to implement; success is often evident only in the long term, and there is no guarantee that deep rooted behavioural problems will be resolved.

It is also important, of course, to ensure that we do not adopt too pessimistic an outlook. Many teachers work hard to raise the self-esteem of these young people by providing learning climates where all achievements are celebrated, where everyone is encouraged to attain their full potential. Effective teachers appreciate the importance of therapy but give their primary consideration to designing an appropriate accessible curriculum which caters for the diverse needs of all young people.

Social learning theory

The social learning theory places emphasis on intervention and the possibility of reinforcing both positive and negative behaviour.

Behavioural techniques can be perceived as having an advantage over psychodynamic techniques in that they tend to offer a more transparent methodology for changing unacceptable behaviour. Unacceptable behaviour is identified in the context in which it occurs by undertaking observation. The antecedents or mechanisms which trigger the behaviour are identified, the frequency and nature of the behaviour recorded and the consequences noted. This approach to behavioural difficulties is known as the ABC method – antecedents, behaviour and consequences – and is discussed in many books on behaviour.

Ultimately the basic aim is to modify behaviour, and behaviour modification is therefore one of the interventionist approaches which complements the social learning theory. Stress is placed upon the relationship between behaviour which can be observed, and its relationship to the resulting consequences. There is no attempt made to interpret underlying causes of human behaviour. The main focus is on rewarding acceptable behaviour and ignoring problematic behaviour in a consistent manner. The following scenario presents the process in action.

Scenario 6

A pupil leaves his seat several times during a lesson whenever the teacher's attention is diverted. The teacher always responds with a reprimand but when the pupil stays seated the teacher seldom responds/attends to him. The aim is to persuade the pupil to leave his seat less often. The solution is to reduce the reinforcement (the teacher's attention) of the unacceptable behaviour (moving around classroom) and reinforce the acceptable behaviour (sitting in seat on task). The teacher must give the attention only when the acceptable behaviour is displayed and try if possible to ignore the problem behaviour. Thus the pupil has the attention he is seeking and hopefully his performance in class will improve.

Advocates of behaviour modification also support the use of token economies and pupil contracts. As always, however, one should tread carefully when trying to alter behaviour. These approaches often look neat and offer solutions within a set timescale, but it must always be kept in mind that behaviour has often been established over a fairly long period of time. This means that it cannot be easily changed and it is best to take your time, persevere and be consistent.

Ecosystemic theory

This theory relies upon a commitment to the principle of collaborative working. It assumes that behaviour is viewed holistically and to effect any lasting change, one must consider that behaviour results from the interactions between the disaffected young person and those whom they encounter in a range of different environments, all of which impinge on each other. This involves teachers, parents, other professionals and peers working together.

The challenging behaviour is seen as the product of interactions which take place in a specific context, i.e. the classroom. Ayers *et al.* (1995) focus on the positive benefits of ecosystemic theory in that it inhibits a child deficit explanation of disruptive behaviour.

To successfully apply this theory, all professionals need to work in a partnership in which everyone's skills are recognised and valued. Some level of awareness in relation to how different professional groups operate is vital, as is the need to share an understanding of why some young people's behaviour is disruptive and how professional skills can be brought together in ways which are complementary rather than conflicting. All too often, assumptions are made about the extent to which different professional groups share a similar outlook as far as the needs of disturbed or troubled young people are concerned.

In short, this coming together of minds is dependent on creating continuing professional development opportunities which bring professionals together with the aim of developing more effective joined-up working. Opportunities like this have been to-date thin on the ground and so professionals cannot really be blamed if they continue to adopt fairly entrenched attitudes based on their particular view of the problem. If they are not aware of how different systems operate, then it is easy to see how ecosystemic theory is unlikely to take root. In addition, one must accept that implementing interprofessional approaches also has resourcing implications and this lack of adequate funding may pose barriers which are difficult to overcome. There is also an assumption that the relationships between individuals, particularly between teachers and parents, are positive and the ecosystemic theory is heavily reliant on this being the case. This, of course, is very much open to question and raises some fundamental issues.

SUMMARY

All teachers are not equally effective in managing behaviour. It is important to qualify such a statement by saying that not all schools and teachers experience the same amount of disruptive behaviour and we have to ensure we are comparing like with like. Some schools have more pupils whose behaviour is challenging than others and in these schools the teacher's job can be more stressful and demanding. However, even when teachers work in the same school with the same pupils some are undoubtedly more effective at managing behaviour than others.

Those who are more effective understand that there are no quick fixes or easy solutions. The less effective teachers often focuss on the negatives and proclaim that the behaviour management strategies do not work. In reality it may be their inability to make them work which is the issue.

It is very important for teachers to look at the bigger picture and this involves standing back and reflecting professionally upon the root causes of the disruptive behaviour. There are usually reasons why the behaviour of some young people can be disruptive, and these reasons can be complicated and deep seated. To develop effective practice in relation to managing behaviour, teachers need to pay careful attention to the underpinning theories. This chapter explores three of these theories: psychodynamic, social learning and systemic. Readers are asked to think about these theories and their implications in practice. The aim of this theoretical model is to provide an analytical frame of reference. I have tried to link each theory directly to practice in order to provide some insights into the fundamental question: Why do some young people behave badly? The argument put forward is that an understanding of behavioural theory helps us to answer this question.

Teachers who attain this level of understanding are best placed to respond effectively to the needs of young people who experience social, emotional and behavioural difficulties.

POINTS FOR REFLECTION

1. Most professionals would agree that in relation to resolving behavioural difficulties there are no quick fixes or easy solutions. However, there are strategies which can promote more positive behaviour. Effective professionals utilise these to good effect but some professionals find it difficult to make these strategies work. Why do you think this is the case?

2. There are several theories which can help to explain why some people's behaviour can be challenging. Do these behavioural theories provide a framework for professional reflection and critical analysis? How do these theories relate to practice?

3. Which of the behavioural theories outlined provides the most valuable insights into the challenging behaviour displayed by young people? Does one theory predominate or do you think the theories are interrelated and complementary?

3 Identifying and assessing behaviour

> *Personal ways:* (Sitting at desk) – Sits lifelessly most of the time/sits quietly and meekly/twists about in seat/slips on to floor/climbs about on desk/doesn't seem to understand that she should keep in seat/slumps, lolls about/sits in a sensible way.
>
> **(Stott, 1974)**

Some initial thoughts

Behaviour is complex and to understand fully some young people's behaviour, professionals need to be able to identify clearly and assess the range of interrelated factors which are potential sources of disaffection. This calls for a holistic approach which takes full account of the behavioural context and examines behaviour as a complex concept. In essence, current thinking in relation to assessing behaviour gives priority to the view that each individual is embedded in a number of systems and there are factors within each of these systems which influence and shape behaviour. This approach is based firmly on systemic theory, and it highlights the importance of taking a wide perspective in relation to assessing behaviour.

Such a perspective should consider the potential impact of factors in the home, community and school and calls for multi-professional assessment. Unfortunately, it is still all too often the case that the young person is seen as a parcel moving between professionals who tend to operate in splendid isolation. There is, of course, a great deal of good work taking place and I will touch on this later. However, at the same time, there is no doubt that there is still a considerable amount of work to be done to achieve the real partnership between professionals which is now advocated as the cornerstone of effective professional partnership. This collaborative focus is given high priority within the *Code of Practice* (SE, 2005) which outlines best practice in supporting children's learning. The *Code of Practice* sets out guidance on the Education (Additional Support for Learning) (Scotland) Act 2004 in relation to assessment of additional support needs. It recommends the development of an integrated assessment system for professionals working with children and young people across education, health, social work services and other areas.

This has not always been the philosophy which has underpinned practice and before moving forward it is important to look briefly at traditional approaches which have not been so enlightened. The aim is not simply to return to the past, but to show how thinking has evolved as professionals have become more effective at understanding and responding to the individual needs of young people who experience social, emotional and behavioural difficulties.

Traditional approaches

For much of the twentieth century emphasis was placed upon categorisation and treatment. The medical model was predominant and the purpose of assessment was to label young people and then devise techniques to modify behaviour or to alter it through therapeutic intervention. This approach dominated professional thinking for much of the twentieth century and to understand fully and appreciate how it shaped current thinking, one must view the evolving process from an historical perspective.

In 1912, the views of the most eminent educational writers and thinkers were brought together in the publication entitled *The Teachers' Encyclopaedia*. This series of seven volumes explored the theory, methods, practice and development of education and covered a wide range of relevant topics. Volume 5, chapter XIX focused upon young people deemed to be in need of 'methods of education suitable for certain classes of children unfitted by various defects affecting mental competence from participating in the school curriculum of their normal fellows' (Laurie, 1912, p. 214).

It was clear that these eminent educationalists gave little or no thought to the possibility that the curriculum was a potential source of behavioural difficulty. They were solely concerned with the classification of young people 'affected by moral abnormality' (Laurie, 1912, p. 224). This theme was also very evident in the thinking which underpinned the 1913 Mental Deficiency Act which described young people who displayed disruptive behaviour as moral defectives, and for the next 30 years or so concepts such as emotional instability and psychological disturbance prevailed.

It was not until 1945 with the publication of the Handicapped Pupils and School Health Regulations that the label 'maladjusted' entered the professional vocabulary. For the first time, young people were referred to as 'maladjusted' which meant they showed evidence of emotional instability and required special educational treatment in order to readjust socially, personally and educationally. In 1955 the *Underwood Report of the Committee on Maladjusted Children* refined the definition of maladjustment by highlighting that such a young person was developing in ways that have a bad effect on himself or his fellows and who cannot, without help, be remedied by his parents, teachers and other adults in ordinary contact with him (MoE, 1955).

Furlong (1985) presents some very interesting and informative statistics which show how quickly the concept of maladjustment took root. Over the fifteen-year period from the publication of the Handicapped Pupils and School Health Regulations in 1945 until 1975 the numbers of young people categorised as maladjusted rose from 0 to 13,000. Laslett (1983) also provides evidence to support the expansion of this group of young people. He gives statistics in relation to how provision also grew to meet the needs of those deemed to be maladjusted. In 1947 there were four residential schools catering for 94 young people and one day school catering for 45 young people. A very different picture emerges in 1980 when there were 120 residential schools and 90 day schools. These figures do not include independent schools or day pupils attending residential schools. Suffice to say, therefore, that over this period of time maladjustment was a growth industry. Wearmouth and Cole (2004) raise a very pertinent point in relation to these developments when they suggest that there is a danger that creating categories such as maladjustment may simply have led to the need to find individuals to fit the category. They quote the work of Mehan (1996) who indicated that categories have a tendency to float around searching for individuals to label and 'gobble up'. This cautionary note must always be kept in mind.

As well as looking at the traditional assessment techniques, one must also think about the professionals who were responsible for undertaking the assessment. Teachers were not really involved in the assessment process. They were more likely to be the ones seeking the advice and guidance of the professionals, such as psychiatrists and psychologists, who were perceived to be the specialists in the field. At this time the Child Guidance Clinic emerged as the working context for these specialists who assessed and worked with the young people referred to them. The psychological service as we now know it was at this time in its infancy. The main message to be grasped is that little or no real attention was placed on the impact of factors which resided in the school system such as the curriculum, teaching style, methodology and organisation.

Assessors used behaviour-specific rating scales to quantify behaviour, while the psychologists focused more on problems residing within the individual. The focus on the individual alone and omission of external factors helps to clarity the inadequacy of these approaches and why a change in thinking was urgently needed.

The inadequacy of the deficit model of assessment

The 1970s proved to be an important decade in relation to changing professional perceptions regarding the nature and range of factors which had an impact on young people who displayed challenging behaviour. Research in the field of behavioural difficulties (Hargreaves et al., 1975; Rutter et al., 1979) began to pinpoint the fact that the experiences provided by schools could either alleviate or exacerbate disruptive behaviour. Tizard (1973) indicated that the nature, range and duration of maladjusted behaviour could be affected by the extent to which the school operated as a socially inclusive community. This was in direct contrast to previous approaches which explained challenging behaviour in terms of deficiencies which resided exclusively within the individual. From this viewpoint the young person was considered to be either mad or bad, requiring sustained medical based intervention or punishment. Bridgeland (1971) and Lloyd and Munn (1999) make the point that the assessment process involved in identifying social, emotional and behavioural difficulties must be carefully considered, as inherent within this concept is the potential to make value judgements. Lloyd and Munn sum up the situation clearly when they say 'experts can tend to assume a deficit model of the child rather than considering the social and organisational circumstances in which the problem occurs' (Lloyd and Munn, 1999, p. 165).

Before considering how the move away from the individual deficit model has influenced assessment practice it is important to look at some of the traditional assessment tools which were used fairly extensively in the past. These rating scales and behavioural questionnaires provide valuable insights into the thinking which underpinned their development and usage. Two widely used rating scales are 'A Children's Behaviour Questionnaire for Completion by Teachers' (Rutter, 1967) and *The Bristol Social Adjustment Guides* (Stott, 1974). In his book *Changing Perceptions of Maladjusted Children (1945–1981)* (1983), Laslett referred to these assessment tools, which at that time were still perceived to be useful indicators of maladjusted behaviour. He indicated that there was evidence of a shift in thinking away from the deficit philosophy but, to a large extent, the assessment emphasis still revolved around a medical model. The following tables provide examples which give some insight into the nature and range of items included in these behavioural rating scales.

A Children's Behaviour Questionnaire				
Statement	Doesn't apply	Applies somewhat	Certainly applies	Anti-social/ Neurotic
Often destroys own or others' belongings				
Has stolen things on more than one occasion				
Often worried about many things				
Often appears miserable, unhappy, tearful or distressed				

(Rutter, 1967)

In total there were 26 descriptive statements of children's behaviour and the assessor was expected to rate these according to the three headings in the grid. If the score fell below nine, the young person was regarded as having adjustment problems. In addition there was a subscale which indicated if the young person was anti-social or neurotic.

Bristol Social Adjustment Guides
Interaction with Teacher
Greeting teacher – Waits to be noticed/hails teacher loudly/ greets normally/can be surly/never thinks of greeting/is too unaware of people to greet
Truthfulness – Always or nearly always truthful/tells fantastic tales/lies from timidity/lies without any compunction
Physique
Physical appearance – attractive/not so attractive/as most/looks undernourished/has some abnormal features.
Physical defects – Bad eyesight/squint/bulging eyes/poor hearing, clumsy, gawky/contorted features.

(Stott, 1974)

These adjustment guides focused upon seven areas:

1 interaction with teacher
2 school work
3 games and play
4 attitude to other children
5 personal ways
6 physique
7 school achievement.

Under each of the seven headings there were a series of descriptive phrases and the assessor was expected to underline the one which in his/her opinion applied most frequently. To give the reader some idea of how this operated I have included some examples of the phrases used under (1) and (6) above. Having rated the behaviours, the assessor could use the manual provided in conjunction with the scores to calculate the extent of the young person's reaction in social situations and ultimately make a decision in relation to the degree of maladjustment.

It is always easy with hindsight to see the pitfalls which are now obvious to the more enlightened professional. One must take care, however, not to discredit the developmental work traditionally undertaken. The contribution of people like Stott and Rutter must be viewed within the historical context in which they worked, and at the time their work most certainly helped to enhance our understanding. However, we can see now that there were flaws in these assessment methods mainly due to the fact that they tended to focus exclusively on individual behavioural defects. Some of the weaknesses inherent in this form of assessment are as follows:

- the label maladjustment assumed that there was a 'norm' to which young people should conform and this 'norm' was understood and shared by all professionals
- little account was taken of the fact that often the behavioural difficulties identified were transient and the young person labelled as maladjusted today may not be described in this way a few weeks later
- decisions about what constitutes maladjusted behaviour were to some extent based upon value judgements. There was a danger that a young person could be described as deviant when in reality the behaviour displayed could be seen to be a logical response to the situation they found themselves in
- there was a lack of attention given to the behavioural context. A young person's behaviour may be heavily influenced by the situational factors and behaviour might be identified as disturbed at home but not at school and vice versa
- important school-based factors tend to be ignored, e.g. the curriculum, classroom organisation, teaching style, resources, teacher–pupil relationships, management styles and peer interactions.

Thus as we moved forward into the twenty-first century it became obvious that if we were going to provide the additional support needed for those whose behaviour was challenging, a much more interactive holistic perspective was required.

A different perspective

The role of the teacher

Professionals must at all times put the young person at the centre of the assessment process. It is important to keep in mind that for some young people whose behaviour is disturbed, there may be a significant inherited or constitutional explanation for this. Some young people may experience mental health problems which underpin their challenging behaviour. They could have psychiatric conditions or have inherited genetic or biological difficulties (Cole *et al.*, 1998). Schools must always be vigilant and seek the advice and support of other professionals in the extended support team such as the health or psychological service, and it is important to know when there is need of specialist help. Having said this, however, teachers must be wary about passing the process of assessing behaviour to others who are not actually in a position to understand and appreciate life in the school and classroom context. Davie (1993, p. 58) sums this up by saying that 'it is important that teachers hold on to the dynamic developmental concept and process of assessment because without it assessment is in some danger of being hijacked by experts'. Teachers must, therefore, take a central role in the process of assessment as they are largely the professionals who experience challenging behaviour at first hand.

Over the last decade there has been a gradual shift away from a narrow psychometric approach dominated by professionals who have a vital role to play as part of the overall team, but who are able only to appear infrequently and who do not always have the time to grasp the full picture. They can really only hope to have a snapshot of the behavioural context and there has undoubtedly been a move away from this narrow focus. This external assessment model no longer predominates and most psychologists are now well aware of the need to assess behaviour in the context in which it occurs. However, even now, psychologists can be perceived by teachers as preferring to work with and assess young people's needs in one-to-one situations outwith classrooms. Teachers rarely have the opportunity to meet with the psychologist who can all too often be seen as making decisions without appreciating the reality of classroom life. This can have an adverse effect on the quality of information passing between professionals because of the lack of positive interaction. In addition it often results in giving those who know the child best a secondary role and this has an impact on the way professionals value each other's contribution. There is still a vital role for the psychologist and there can be little doubt that the team of psychologists who provide psychological services to schools is usually stretched to the limits and under-resourced. Nonetheless, teachers must be given the time and opportunity to play a more prominent and influential role in the assessment process. They need to be able to stand back and observe behaviour in the classroom context, taking account of the range of factors affecting it and appreciating that to understand it fully they need to see behaviour as a wide-ranging concept.

Observing behaviour

The topic of observation as an assessment tool is wide ranging and involves the consideration of many issues and ideas. It is not my intention here to go into this in detail. If the reader is interested in enhancing their knowledge, there are several informative books which will provide a more comprehensive coverage, for instance, Fawcett (1996) and Sharma *et al.* (2000). For those who may be interested in using observation as a means of more detailed classroom research, Simpson and Tuson (2003) provide a good reference point.

While I support completely the view expressed by Nisbet (1977, p. 15) that 'observation is a highly skilled activity for which an extensive knowledge and understanding is required', and agree that in terms of formal research studies one must think very carefully before proceeding, my aim is to provide the busy professional with a way to assess challenging behaviour as an integral part of the teaching and learning process. What is being proposed must be able to fit in with this ongoing process and not be something additional which creates an extra burden. At this level, observation is to be seen as a natural part of the teacher's job and as a skill teachers are well able to develop.

Teachers are understandably interested in practical approaches which they can utilise in classrooms. I would therefore recommend the following two resources which focus on observation in a way which is accessible to the teacher:

1 Ayers *et al.* (2006) *Assessing Individual Needs – A Practical Approach* (2nd edn) London: David Fulton

2 Hull Learning Services (2005) *Supporting Children with Behavioural Difficulties* London: David Fulton

Both resources touch on the ABC approach as a useful way of structuring observation. This refers to the Antecedents (events prior to the actual behaviour), the Behaviour (the actual behaviour observed) and Consequences (the result/effect of the behaviour). As I have said there is a lot to effective observation which is beyond the scope of this chapter and teachers who wish to learn more can use the above resources as a starting point. Ayers (2006) makes a distinction between formal and informal observation:

- formal observation consists of using an observation schedule that enables the observer to quantify the pupil's behaviour
- informal observation consists of making notes of the pupil's behaviour without quantifying or counting them.

Classroom teachers have to exist in the real world and classrooms are busy places where teachers have to cater for the needs of a diverse group of learners. I would suggest that teachers are more likely to be able to put into action informal observation and therefore I have produced a sample of an observation schedule which might be helpful. This schedule is by no means exhaustive and the teacher will be able to identify aspects which could be added. This is simply my version of what an informal schedule might cover. It provides a broad overview of the nature of the behaviour and the context in which it occurs and will, I hope, provide a useful reference point for the teacher who wishes to understand more fully the challenging behaviour exhibited by a young person.

Observation schedule 1

The Curriculum

Is the curriculum on offer appropriate and accessible?

Is there evidence of differentiation catering for diversity in learner ability?

Are the resources used well presented/at a suitable level/ stimulating/interesting?

Are tasks clearly understood by the learners? Are they well paced/challenging?

Is the range and variety of tasks acceptable?

What is produced and how does it compare to what was expected?

What forms of assessment are used? Are they suited to the learners' needs?

Is the learning environment stimulating and motivating?

Is the classroom organisation conducive to effective teaching/ learning?

Are the lessons well planned, prepared and delivered?

The Observed Pupil

Does the observed pupil interact positively/negatively with his/her peers?

How does he/she react in group situations?

What strengths are evident which could be built on?

Can this pupil work independently?

Does he/she demand attention? If so, under what circumstances?

Are there times when the behaviour is acceptable? When/how does this happen?

Does the pupil have learning difficulties? What is the nature/range of these difficulties?

What support is available? Is it appropriate and targeted?

Does the pupil interact with the teacher? If not, why not?

Is the pupil involved in plans/decisions which impact on him/her?

Does the pupil have a preferred learning style?

The Teacher

Has the task/activity been explained clearly?

Does the teacher try to interact with the pupil? What is the response?

Does the teacher actively encourage the pupil to answer questions/volunteer information?

Is the teacher's use of language appropriate?

Does the teacher use a range of teaching styles/methodologies?

Does the teacher adopt a deficit or a curricular philosophy?

Is the teacher interested in the pupil's views/ideas and interests?

What is the teacher's dominant management style?

Does the teacher make an effort to enhance the pupil's self-esteem?

Is the teacher aware of the impact of the hidden curriculum?

Is praise and encouragement utilised whenever possible?

Does the teacher make time to listen to the pupil?

It is also very important to remember that in our efforts to ensure we are avoiding a deficit approach, we do not assume that this means we cannot focus more specifically on the particular behaviours displayed by an individual, as long as we set our observations in the wider context discussed above. To give the teacher a more comprehensive picture and to target areas effectively for development, a more personally focused observation schedule should prove to be helpful. Hill and Parsons (2000) have developed some excellent resources which would help the teacher develop a needs analysis approach. I would refer the reader to this material and reproduce on the following page a slightly adapted extract from their behaviour questionnaire.

Observation schedule 2

Use the rating scale to indicate the extent of behaviour displayed by the pupil in terms of level of difficulty. In the comments column provide additional information about the behavioural context, antecedents and consequences.

1 extremely difficult 2 very difficult 3 difficult 4 not too difficult 5 not an issue

Type of behaviour	1	2	3	4	5	Comments
Hindering/annoying other pupils						
Making unnecessary, non-verbal noises						
Persistently infringing school and/or class rules						
Getting out of seat without permission						
Verbal abuse towards other pupils						
Cheeky and/or impertinent remarks or responses						
Damage to own work or work of others						
Talking out of turn						
Lack of concern for others						
Unruliness while waiting to enter classrooms or queuing for lunch						
General rowdiness, horseplay or mucking about						
Physical aggression towards other pupils						
Verbal abuse towards you or other staff members						
Physical aggression towards you or other staff members						

Hill and Parsons (2000)

The way forward

As we move into the twenty-first century three areas of good assessment practice relating to behaviour consistently emerge as key factors. First, it is becoming clear that young people themselves should take a more prominent part in the assessment process which, after all, significantly affects them. Second, information obtained via the assessment process is useful only in as far as it is translated into an individual educational plan. Third, there is a need to recognise that for many young people who display social, emotional and behavioural difficulties there are likely to be other professionals involved and this calls for a co-ordinated multi-agency approach.

Involving the young person

Article 12 of the UN Convention on the Rights of the Child (1990), to which the UK government is a signatory, makes it very clear that all young people have the right to express their view in relation to matters which have an impact on their lives.

The *Better Behaviour – Better Learning* report (SEED, 2001) stresses the importance of actively involving young people and ensuring their voice is heard. The report focuses on young people who may be disaffected and excluded and places emphasis upon the fact that when these young people feel included as part of the process, their behaviour becomes more positive and challenging behaviour is significantly reduced.

There is clear evidence that developments in relation to involving young people are bearing some fruit, and there are now many schools that have put in place school councils as a forum for young people to express their views. However, there is still a long way to go if the rhetoric is to become reality. Many young people continue to remain silent and are not in a position to influence the policies and practices which shape their lives. This is particularly true of young people who are disadvantaged and disaffected.

One group of young people who are often excluded from schools and consequently have little or no say in decisions which have a major impact on them, are those whose behaviour is deemed to be disruptive. According to Hamill and Boyd (2000) these young people are often on the receiving end of the decision-making process because they have difficulty in developing social competence, adjusting to social contexts and in learning to follow normal and accepted behaviour patterns.

Professionals thus need to make a special effort to involve this particular group and this may pose particular challenges. One vital part of the decision-making process is assessment. At this stage of the process very important information is being gathered, and in order to bring to the process validity and authenticity it is vital that young people have their say, and this must be built in at this initial stage.

Multi-agency collaboration

The idea of multi-agency planning and inter-professional partnership is now high on the educational agenda. This collaborative approach was highlighted in 1998 in circular 2/98 published by the Scottish Office Education and Industry Department which focused on the issue of school exclusions. It highlighted that 'good inter agency co-operation improves efficiency, and effectiveness; reduces frustration between professionals from different disciplines and makes better use of existing resources' (SOEID, 1998, p. 18). This theme is at the heart of the legislation which underpins policy and practice in the field of additional support needs and is a central aspect which recurs consistently in the document *Supporting Children's Learning: Code of Practice* (SE, 2005). The concept of multi-agency collaboration is seen as one of the key factors in relation to meeting additional support needs.

Young people whose behaviour is disruptive and who may also experience social and emotional difficulties are now considered to have additional support needs and so it is important to ensure that their needs are considered holistically, as often they are involved with a number of different agencies. In relation to assessment it is therefore necessary to ensure that all contributing factors are considered and to do this effectively will involve a multidisciplinary approach.

It is not uncommon to hear some young people being described as 'high tariff' in terms of the severity of the disruptive behaviour they display. These young people often come from dysfunctional families, are psychologically disturbed and cause problems at home in the community and at school. They are usually known to a range of agencies and have input from a range of professionals such as education, social work, health, community education, psychological services and the police. However, all of this input has often in the past remained fragmented and there was insufficient attention paid to developing a joined-up approach.

In these circumstances there may be a need to set up a co-ordinated support plan. The nature and purpose of these plans are fully explained in *Supporting Children's Learning: Code of Practice* (SE, 2005). The co-ordinated support plan is a statutory document which is subject to regular monitoring and review. It has implications for the assessment process, particularly for young people who present disturbed behaviour which challenges all relevant professionals to work as a team.

SUMMARY

To understand current thinking in relation to the assessment and identification of behaviour it is necessary to adopt a historical perspective. Traditional approaches have focused almost exclusively upon a system of labelling where individuals were described as maladjusted. This concept of maladjustment dominated thinking for most of the twentieth century and the prime aim of assessing behavioural difficulties was to focus on the individual's inbuilt deficiencies. No account was taken of factors such as the curriculum, teaching style, methodology, relationships or ethos. The psychologist was the dominant professional and use was made of rating scales to assess behaviour according to a number of restricted criteria.

In the latter half of the century things began to change. It was gradually acknowledged that to appreciate fully the reasons for misbehaviour, it was vital to take full account of the context in which it occurred. As a result, behaviour became better understood as a relationship issue.

In order to gain this more comprehensive overview it was necessary to observe behaviour *in situ*. Thus observation emerged as a more appropriate assessment tool which led to a better grasp of the root causes of indiscipline. The role of the teacher was also given higher priority and it became clear that teachers were in a unique position to observe and record behavioural issues.

In the future, young people themselves will continue to be encouraged to play a more prominent role in relation to the assessment process and they should have a voice in relation to the decisions which affect them. In addition, good assessment practice will become characterised by multi-agency collaboration, bringing the full range of relevant professionals together as an extended assessment team. The assessment process will be more collaborative, holistic and child-centred.

POINTS FOR REFLECTION

1 Traditional approaches to the assessment of behavioural difficulties emphasised the need for categorisation and treatment. A medical model prevailed with a strong emphasis on labels such as 'maladjusted'. Have professionals now totally rejected this deficit approach to the assessment of disruptive behaviour?

2 Does observation as outlined in this chapter now feature highly as an assessment tool in relation to identifying the factors which can influence behaviour? Have professionals now internalised a more systemic holistic approach when assessing behaviour which can be challenging?

3 Are young people whose behaviour is disruptive seen as an integral part of the behavioural assessment process? Should they be allowed to voice their views in relation to the factors they perceive as having an impact on their behaviour? Are their views valid and, if so, who is listening to them?

4 Inclusion can be challenging

‘ Some aspects of the broad inclusion agenda present particularly difficult challenges to schools and education authorities. ’

(HMIE, 2002)

Setting the context

For most of the twentieth century, professionals who worked with and supported young people accepted without question that some individuals were not deemed capable of being educated in mainstream schools. They were assessed as having a deficiency which prevented them from benefiting from the systems set up for the majority of their peers, who were considered to meet the educational norms laid down by an educational system which operated according to the principles of categorisation, stereotyping and segregation. Signs of change only really began to emerge in the last decade of the twentieth century, and the initial discussion focused upon the need to reintegrate some young people into mainstream schools. It is important to point out that at this time integration was related to disability and the word integration came to have meaning only when applied to those labelled as having special educational needs, who were segregated.

Integration is now largely an obsolete term and it only has meaning in systems which encourage segregation and exclusion. The emphasis is now placed on inclusion which is at the heart of educational policy, at least in theory. Central to this theoretical perspective is the principle of rights which is enshrined in the *Salamanca Statement and Framework for Action on Special Educational Needs* as follows:

Regular schools with this inclusive orientation are the most effective means of combating discriminatory attitudes, creating welcoming communities, building an inclusive society and achieving education for all: moreover they provide an effective education to the majority of children and improve the efficiency and ultimately the cost effectiveness of the entire education system.

(UNESCO, 1994, p. ix)

The Centre for Studies in Inclusive Education (CSIE) gives priority to the right of all young people to participate in the life and work of the mainstream institutions to the best of their abilities, whatever their needs. This ideological perspective is given high priority within the ongoing inclusion debate. Few disagree with it in theory and many teachers continue to agree with the principle but dispute the practicalities, which they see as continuing to pose barriers to inclusion. Before examining what some of these barriers might be, it is important to understand the rationale which underpins the inclusive ideology and then go on to consider the practical implications which must be addressed if inclusion is to become the reality envisaged in the Salamanca statement.

Inclusion education in principle

There can be few people who would argue with the principles underpinning inclusion. Who would dispute the view expressed by Thomas *et al.* (1998) when they convey inclusion as being at the core of a civilised society which values all citizens equally and which gives high priority to promoting human rights issues. Inclusion must take centre stage in a society which embraces a liberal and pluralistic culture; one that celebrates and promotes fraternity and equality of opportunity. At the heart of inclusion is the premise that it will encourage a culture which celebrates diversity and recognises the need to set up inclusive systems, at all levels of society, which are able to combat social disadvantage and eradicate the difficulties associated with social exclusion. A wealth of literature now exists in relation to the field of inclusion, and an increasing number of academics are writing about inclusive education such as Ainscow (1999), Mittler (2000), Nind *et al.* (2003), and Topping and Maloney (2005).

Throughout all of this literature, a series of themes consistently re-occurs which conveys the essence of inclusion in action:

- catering for diversity
- developing potential
- opportunity for all
- equality of value
- achievement for all
- human rights
- overcoming barriers
- social justice
- combating disadvantage
- partnership, participation and collaboration
- restructuring cultures
- fostering mutually sustaining relationships.

Mittler (2000) in particular, makes an extremely interesting point when he suggests that inclusion is a powerful force which should be harnessed by schools, because it has the potential to transform them so that they become environments which provide genuine social and educational opportunities for all. Other writers have also taken up this point and much of the current literature emphasises the inherent capacity of inclusion to change schools for the better, by encouraging them to be innovative in relation to restructuring traditional approaches to learning and teaching, thus making them more responsive to a much wider range of learner need. The prime focus is upon the right of the young person to be educated in the mainstream school and in Scotland this is now enshrined in law. The Standards in Scotland's Schools Etc. Act 2000 gives priority, at least in principle, to what it calls the presumption of mainstreaming. However, young people can still be excluded if the following criteria apply:

- the mainstream school would not be suited to the ability or aptitude of the child
- where a child's attendance at the mainstream school would be incompatible with the provision of an effective education for his/her peers
- if the placement resulted in unreasonable public expenditure.

It is clear, therefore, that although the principle is now firmly in place, it is still possible in law to exclude certain young people in exceptional circumstances if these conditions apply.

One organisation which places inclusion at the heart of education is the Centre for Studies in Inclusive Education which was established in 1996. The Centre opposes all forms of exclusion and sees any form of specialist provision outwith mainstream as violating students' rights. This organisation commissioned a report in 2002 written by Sharon Rustemier and entitled *Social and Educational Justice – The Human Rights Framework for Inclusion*. This report questions the continuing philosophical, financial and legislative support for segregated schooling and claims that segregated schooling is still alive and well, and that, internationally, such education marginalises young people and can be seen to be discriminatory. According to Rustemier, segregated schooling breaches all four principles which are at the centre of the 1990 UN Convention on the Rights of the Child.

The CSIE sees inclusive education as good education and with its focus on human rights, it makes good sense to include all regardless of their perceived abilities or disabilities. The following table outlines the reasons given by CSIE to support inclusion. These reasons are underpinned by a set of principles based on human rights, effective education and social interaction.

Human rights
All children have the right to learn together.
Children should not be devalued/discriminated against by being excluded because of their disability or learning/behavioural difficulty.
There are no legitimate reasons to separate children for their education. Children belong together with advantages/benefits for everyone. They do not need to be protected from each other.
Disabled adults describing themselves as special school survivors are demanding an end to segregation.

Effective education
Children do better academically and socially in inclusive settings.
Given commitment and support, inclusive education is a more efficient use of resources.
There is no teaching or care which cannot take place in a mainstream school.
Segregation teaches children to be fearful, ignorant and breeds prejudice.
All children need an education that will help them develop relationships and prepare them for the reality of life.
Only inclusion has the potential to reduce fear and build friendship, respect and understanding.

(CSIE, inclusion.uwe.ac.uk/csie/10rsns.htm)

Cigman (2007) argues that the CSIE takes a radical position on inclusion and sees all forms of segregation as totally unjustified, morally reprehensible and ruining lives. A counter-argument is now presented by Mary Warnock, often seen as one of the first to promote inclusive education. In 2005, she revisited her original report and concluded that she now wished to reconsider 'what is possibly the most disastrous legacy of the 1978 report, the concept of inclusion (formerly known as integration)' (Warnock, 2005, p. 22).

Warnock now presents a more moderate approach to inclusion and sees inclusive education as relating to that educational environment which meets the child's needs as opposed to pushing the ideology that inclusion equates to mainstreaming. Thus it is clear that the debate concerning inclusion is still alive and well. Few people would argue against democracy and in the same way, few would reject inclusion out of hand.

It is not difficult to embrace wholeheartedly the principle of inclusion and in 2000 the Standards in Scotland's Schools Etc. Act identified inclusion as one of five national priorities and described its vision as follows:

Inclusion and Equality: to promote equality and help every pupil benefit from education, with particular regard paid to pupils with disabilities and special educational needs, and to Gaelic and other lesser used languages.

(www.nationalpriorities.org.uk)

Translating principles into practice is not an easy matter. The vast majority of teachers have no problem internalising the principle of inclusion. However, they perceive a range of issues which present barriers to inclusion and which, all too often, are not fully addressed in the ideological drive towards inclusion. These barriers will be considered in the next section. The aim is not to reject inclusion, but to ensure that those who advocate inclusion do not underestimate the inherent challenges which must be faced. Setting a priority is not the same thing as ensuring the priority translates into action.

Inclusion – facing the challenge

It is very important to ensure that all voices are heard in relation to inclusion and although some authors tend to adopt an ideological stance this can all too often result in less emphasis being placed on highlighting and subjecting to critical scrutiny potential barriers to inclusion. There are, of course, some authors who are critical of what they perceive to be the zealous promotion of inclusion often advocated by the armchair inclusionist. These individuals often have little experience of the reality of school life. They write with conviction about the theory of inclusion without having to actually put the ideal into practice. We must adopt a critically analytic approach to what Bailey (1998) describes as the fervent crusade promoting inclusive schooling. Low (1997) cautions against an uncritical approach and some authors are now calling for responsible inclusion as opposed to pushing for full inclusion at all cost.

Farrell (2004) highlights the potential dangers in setting the drive for inclusion within a human rights agenda and O'Brien (2001) encourages us to put the child's needs to the fore as the prime factor in determining the best learning environment rather than focusing on the one size fits all approach. It must be emphasised that there is still a considerable on-going debate surrounding inclusion. Teachers are well aware of this and from my experience of working with them on a number of continuing professional development courses, the majority fully support inclusion in principle but feel they have justifiable concerns which are not taken on board. Many feel inclusion is being forced on them and they have little ownership of this initiative. They accept that they will need to make adjustments and most are doing so. However, they continue to express reservations at the way their concerns are dismissed. There are barriers which must be acknowledged and overcome if inclusion is to move from principle into practice.

Raising attainment

Over the past twenty years there has been an increasing commitment within the education system to improving standards for all learners. Throughout the late 1980s and into the 1990s a great deal of research went into identifying the features of an effective school. Two important reports written by SOED in 1989 (*Effective Primary Schools*) and 1988 (*Effective Secondary Schools*) highlighted the characteristics of good practice found in both primary and secondary schools. One theme that was prioritised was the fundamental role played by schools in promoting learning environments where all learners have the opportunity to realise their potential.

There was also evidence of a gradual move towards modernising the curriculum. For example, the 5–14 guidelines (SOED, 1994) which provided a curricular framework have been extremely influential in developing a curriculum for young people in the 5–14 years age range. Again a strong emphasis was placed upon the need to raise attainment.

In 1996, in the report *Achievement for All*, SOEID recommended that all schools should 'include an examination of standards of attainment in their development plans and set targets for improvement' (SOEID, 1996, p. 33).

The most recent educational development is enshrined in the Curriculum for Excellence programme which was published in 2004. It sets out for the first time values, purposes and principles for the 3–18 curriculum for all young people. The aim of the proposed curricular framework is to develop successful learners, confident individuals, responsible citizens and effective contributors. Although this new framework aims to be more flexible and innovative, it still has at its heart the need for all learners to achieve to their full potential.

It is within this culture of quality with its developing ethos of attainment that the concept of 'additional support needs' has evolved. This new concept replaces the term 'special educational needs' and it is now clear that a much more diverse range of learners are now deemed to have additional support needs. Traditionally, the majority of these learners would have been educated in some form of segregated provision and the mainstream school was not considered an appropriate context in which their needs might be met. However, there has also been a major shift in the philosophy which underpinned these preconceptions, and just as the concept of additional support needs has slowly evolved, so too has the shift away from segregation towards inclusion.

There have been two parallel developments evident over the past twenty years or so. On the one hand, the drive towards raising attainment for all, and the move away from segregation to inclusive education on the other. Many teachers still question the extent to which these twin developments are compatible, given the levels of resourcing and support necessary to enable teachers to make both a reality. Scenario 1 illustrates this point.

Scenario 1

Mrs Smith has a primary 7 class of 28 pupils. She is a keen enthusiastic teacher who is committed to the principle of inclusion. She tries her best to cater for a diverse range of needs within her classroom and makes a real effort to provide an appropriate differentiated curriculum for all. She has two children who are dyslexic; one who has AD/HD and takes Ritalin; one child who is looked after and displays very challenging behaviour; and one child who has Down's Syndrome and hearing difficulties. In addition there are two children who are at 5–14 level A in relation to literacy and numeracy. The dyslexic children are withdrawn from class for one hour per week by the support for learning teacher for help with reading; she also works in class for one hour per week supporting the level A pupils. A specialist comes in for one hour every week to support the child with Down's Syndrome. The head teacher asked Mrs Smith to come and see her because she felt some of the more able children were not achieving the targets set for them and she was concerned about how the school would rank in the league tables which would be published in due course.

Resourcing/funding

There can be no doubt that effective inclusion is dependent upon the provision of adequate resources. Despite the claim by the government and the local authorities that they have increased resourcing, the reality in schools is that many teachers perceive the lack of appropriate resourcing as a major obstacle to the implementation of inclusion.

In 2000 and 2003 Hamill and Boyd undertook research in two local authorities in Scotland. As part of this research, over 1500 secondary and primary teachers were asked for their views in relation to inclusion. A constantly recurring theme was the widely held belief that not only was inclusion totally underfunded but, in addition, many teachers thought that it was a politically motivated initiative aimed more at cost-cutting than meeting need. Hamill and Boyd noted that many teachers felt their local authority was not providing adequate funding, and there was a perception that resources were being held back. However, this was not the case in reality and each authority was making every effort to ensure resources were made available. The authorities could only work with the resources they received, and it was clear that, in fact, making inclusion work required a much higher level of funding than was available to them. Scenario 2 illustrates this point.

Scenario 2

David currently attends a special school. He is physically disabled and uses a wheelchair. He also has moderate learning difficulties in relation to both literacy and numeracy. He is currently in primary 4 and his parents now feel he would be better placed in his local mainstream primary school and want him to move there next session. They are particularly concerned that the special school is some distance away and this is hampering David's social and emotional development as he is cut off from his able-bodied friends who attend the local primary. There are issues regarding access as the mainstream school is, as it stands, not physically suited to David's needs. In short, a considerable amount of finance will be required to adapt the school for David. The local authority feels that the special school is already fully adapted and David's needs are being met effectively in that context.

Resourcing is, of course, a much more complex issue than simply providing materials and equipment. It is about ensuring teachers are given the necessary opportunities to undertake continuing professional development (CPD) in relation to meeting a more diverse range of learning needs. This CPD is needed at two levels: first, for the classroom teacher who is increasingly expected to include young people with a range of needs and who feels inadequately prepared to meet the challenges involved; second, there is a need to provide more intensive specialist training for those teachers who will become support for learning teachers or those who will work in special provision outwith the mainstream. At the moment most local authorities do their best to provide this CPD but unfortunately too many teachers continue to feel that their best is not good enough. Teachers have the same right as their pupils to feel supported and there is an urgent need to provide the

CPD opportunities which will help teachers feel better equipped to deal with the challenges inherent in the drive towards inclusion. Scenario 3 illustrates this point.

Scenario 3

Richard is a child with severe social, emotional and behavioural difficulties (SEBD). He has been placed in a behavioural unit outwith the mainstream school for two mornings a week. His class teacher has been told he will get specialist support there in a small group or on a one-to-one basis. He is in her primary 6 class of 25 pupils in the mainstream school for the rest of the week and she has to provide support for him on her own. She does her best but realises she needs some training in relation to meeting the needs of a child with such complex needs. She saw a module offered by the university on this subject and she asked to go. The head teacher wants to support her but says she cannot attend as the school cannot afford the three days staff cover required.

Definition

It is vital to realise that terms such as inclusive education can mean different things to different people. There is not as yet a shared understanding of the terminology and, in fact, teachers, researchers, politicians, bureaucrats and parents may internalise the concept of inclusion very differently. One must start by dispelling the myth that inclusion is one single entity and accept that it is actually a process and that people experience this process differently. To appreciate a person's viewpoint, one must understand the factors which have influenced and shaped it. Ainscow (1999) sees inclusion as a process which reaches out and impacts on the experience of all learners. This approach is summed up by Barton (1997, p. 85) when he says:

> Inclusion is a process. Inclusive education is not merely about providing access into mainstream for pupils who have previously been excluded. Existing school systems – in terms of physical factors, curriculum aspects, teaching expectations and styles, leadership roles – will have to change.

The emphasis is placed on defining inclusion as a diverse concept, which does not focus exclusively upon that group of young people with additional support needs, but extends beyond this to embrace all regardless of ability, gender, sexual orientation, religion, race, social class and linguistic orientation (Booth and Ainscow, 1998). It is, however, important to keep in mind that much of the literature on inclusion has emerged in the context of additional support needs and consequently it often takes as its focus the inclusion of young people with special needs.

Many teachers still perceive inclusion as a concept which relates exclusively to additional support needs (ASN) and view schools as inclusive depending on their ability and willingness to include these young people. The inclusion of ASN pupils is, of course, a major part of the drive towards inclusion, but to perceive it purely in these terms is narrow and restrictive. The belief that schools become inclusive simply because they fit a few children with ASN into their existing structures must be challenged. Fundamentally all professionals need to explore the all-embracing definition of inclusion as having the power to transform schools for the benefit of all learners. Scenario 4 illustrates this point.

Scenario 4

Mr Jones, the headmaster of a secondary school, prides himself on what he describes as his inclusive school. He is often heard emphasising the fact that he has included several young people with social, emotional and behavioural needs, two young people with Down's Syndrome, an autistic child and a physically disabled young person. The support available to them is, in fact, very good. However, in a recent HM Inspection several staff reported that the ethos in the school was fairly negative and they did not feel they had any input into/ownership of the school development plan. The model of management they described was still very much a top-down model without any real attempt to take on board their views, and staff felt that inclusion was imposed on them and they were not included in the decision-making processes within the school. The school leader appeared to have a limited vision in relation to inclusion.

Mainstreaming

A much more diverse range of learning need is now catered for within the mainstream school. Most schools strive to create inclusive cultures where all young people can have opportunities to develop their full potential. However, schools also have to be realistic in relation to how they group pupils so that they can benefit most effectively from the process of effective teaching and learning.

In 1996, in the report *Achievement for All* (SOEID), HM inspectors highlighted the importance of carefully considering the different ways of organising pupils between and within classes and the effects this process has upon learning and teaching. They concluded that the decision about the basis upon which classes should be formed is one of the most important which school managers have to make. This decision can have far-reaching consequences in relation to the extent to which pupils feel included and just because a child is in a mainstream school does not automatically mean she/he is included.

The *Achievement For All* report presented the most common forms of organisation as streaming, setting and mixed ability. Many schools now use streaming and setting as the prime organisational device. This is done in the best interests of all pupils, but for some it can be a device which marginalises them. As a result of this approach, some young people find themselves in the so-called bottom set due to their learning/behavioural difficulties. In reality a sizeable minority of pupils find themselves in colonies or ghettos within schools and remain on the periphery of school life as opposed to being an integral part of the community. This is borne out by the work done by Dyson (1997) who concluded that, to a large extent, children with additional support needs are expected to fit into existing systems and no real effort is made to transform these systems to cater for diversity of need. Scenario 5 illustrates this point.

Scenario 5

Leon has moderate learning difficulties and has been in a special school for the past three years. It is decided that he is now ready to return to the mainstream secondary school. This school uses a system of setting and as Leon has difficulties in both numeracy and literacy he finds himself in the bottom set in all subjects. The composition of this set does not really change as the others in the set have difficulties similar to Leon. In reality this is a remedial class by another name. It represents a segregated colony of learners who have little opportunity to become truly integrated.

Behaviour – an issue for inclusion

In the report *Count Us In* (HMIE, 2002), important messages were conveyed in relation to how inclusion might be effectively achieved in schools. Emphasis was placed upon the complexity of issues which had to be considered in any debate. One particular issue, which was given some priority, was the challenges which surround the needs of those young people who feel alienated and marginalised as a result of their social, emotional and behavioural difficulties which all too often result in disruptive behaviour. The report made it very clear that the needs of this group presented challenges to any school trying to achieve the ideals of inclusive education. It emphasised that 'some aspects of the broad inclusion agenda present particularly difficult challenges to schools and education authorities' (HMIE, 2002, p. 34).

The report also indicated that disruptive behaviour was an issue for inclusion and this was borne out by Hamill and Boyd (2000; 2003) in their research into the inclusion in Scottish schools of young people whose behaviour was challenging. These researchers supported the view that there were specific behaviour-related factors which impacted on the extent to which schools were successful in achieving inclusion. Many of these factors are addressed throughout this book, but at this point I would like to provide some insight into the nature of some fundamental areas of concern. The following three areas represent the concerns most frequently raised by teachers.

1 Additional support needs (special educational needs)

In my opinion pupils whose behaviour is challenging don't have special educational needs; they make the choice to be disruptive and in fact they make things worse for those who genuinely have special needs.

(Teacher)

All too often in the past, young people whose disruptive behaviour resulted from social and emotional difficulties, were not included in that group of young people deemed to have special educational needs (additional support needs). Identifying and meeting these needs can be a complex matter as a great deal still depends upon the perception of what is normal and acceptable behaviour, and these perceptions can vary considerably and be influenced by an individual's experiences.

The Education Act 1993 stated that a young person had special educational needs if he/she had significantly greater difficulty in learning than the majority of children of the same age and if the difficulty called for educational provision which is additional to or different from that made generally for children of the same age. There can be little doubt that young people with social, emotional and behavioural difficulties often experience learning difficulties because they have problems developing social competencies and in internalising appropriate behavioural patterns.

For the past fifteen years it has been recognised, at least in the legislation, that this group of young people do have special educational needs (additional support needs) although many teachers have not found it easy to fit the needs of these young people into the special needs (additional needs) framework, and to some extent this has impacted upon the nature and range of the support which has been provided.

In *Supporting Children's Learning: Code of Practice* (2005), the Scottish Executive (SE) officially brought the needs of these young people from the periphery into the centre of the educational arena. They outlined clearly that additional support needs was a much more diverse concept than traditionally presented, and that many of the circumstances identified as giving rise to additional support were closely linked to the area of social, emotional and behavioral difficulties. Thus, at least in theory, the situation is now clear. However, I would suggest that more work will need to be done in order for some teachers to move away from a fairly restrictive view and to accept thinking which they might find challenges views strongly based upon a deficiency model of learners.

2 Conflict of rights

The rights of the minority who constantly disrupt lessons take precedence over the rights of the majority who behave and want to learn. Their rights are often ignored or relegated to second place.

(Teacher)

Earlier in this chapter, I looked at the principles which underpin the concept of inclusion. One principle which is given priority, is that inclusion is very much a human rights issue and to exclude an individual from mainstream education ultimately results in ignoring their right to social inclusion. This issue of rights becomes more complex when it is applied to young people whose behaviour disrupts the education of others. The studies by Hamill and Boyd found strong evidence to support the view that often there appeared to be a conflict of rights, and this was due to the fact that in many classrooms disruptive young people tended to dominate and take up inappropriate amounts of teacher time. It also has to be said that there was also evidence to suggest that all teachers are not equally skilled at managing this difficult behaviour.

It was clear that the group of learners most affected were those young people who experienced learning difficulties and who often found themselves in the bottom sets with the most disruptive pupils who were not fulfilling their potential due their lack of motivation and disaffection. In addition, teachers also made the case that they were reluctant to include young people whose additional support needs resulted from sensory/physical disabilities in classrooms where they already had to cope with disruptive pupils. Thus the inclusion of those with challenging behaviour was impacting negatively on the inclusion of other vulnerable learners.

A further issue revolves around the parents' right to choose the place where their child should be educated. It is often assumed that all parents want their child in the mainstream sector. This is not necessarily the case and one has to accept that some parents wish to exercise their right to send their child to a special school or unit where they feel that their child's needs will be met in a more conducive learning environment.

Finally, teachers often ask the question, what are our rights? This is linked to a perception that the increase in the numbers of pupils with SEBD has led to health and safety concerns. It also relates to the right of teachers to receive adequate training in understanding and responding to the needs of young people with SEBD. This right is not always given priority and so many teachers feel that they are not adequately prepared for the task.

3 Exclusion

> If a pupil is disruptive they deserve to be excluded – some young people forfeit the right to education. Those who pursue inclusion with a missionary zeal are never on the receiving end of the bad behaviour.
>
> (Teacher)

There is ample research evidence to suggest that when the concept of inclusion focuses upon young people whose behaviour can be challenging and disruptive, the issues become more highly charged (Cooper, 1993; O'Brien, 1998; Porter, 2007). The label 'social, emotional and behavioural difficulties' is applied to a fairly wide range of young people from those who misbehave sporadically and for a relatively short stage in their development to those whose behaviour is more severe and may have more deep-rooted causes. Barber (1996) alludes to a vicious circle which begins with underachievement fuelling disaffection and exclusion leading to detachment from the education system.

These young people pose problems for their schools, and for many teachers the most obvious solution is exclusion, thus compounding the sense of alienation and marginalisation these young people feel. In spite of the fact that inclusion is cited as one of the national priorities, the numbers of young people excluded because of disruptive behaviour is on the increase.

There is evidence to suggest that sometimes these young people are perceived purely in terms of the problems they pose for their schools, teachers and peers. This takes the focus away from the fact that there are also school-based factors outwith the young person's control which contribute towards exclusive practices. Thus, although on the surface schools appear to be more inclusive, in practice, for some young people with SEBD, exclusion is still alive and well.

SUMMARY

Over the past decade or so the concept of inclusion has been high on the educational agenda. Many of those who conduct research in this field and write about inclusion present it as having the power to transform schools for the better. They emphasise the underpinning principles of equality, justice and rights. Others, while still supporting inclusion in principle, do not underestimate the fact that making inclusion a reality can be challenging. These authors question what they see as an ideological stance and insist on subjecting the inclusive process to more critical scrutiny.

Putting the principles of inclusion into practice can pose difficulties. This does not mean we should reduce the drive towards inclusion, but perhaps we need to think more carefully about the barriers to inclusion and how we can break these down. Most teachers have internalised the principle of inclusion but do not always find it easy to translate these principles into practice.

One of the main problems relates to defining inclusion, and it can mean different things to different people. There is still some confusion surrounding it and we must continue to strive to clarify the situation. One of the major issues relates to the link between mainstreaming and inclusion. On the one hand, those who emphasise inclusion as a human right insist that everyone should be educated in the mainstream school. However, those who are less likely to support this ideological stance argue that young people should be educated in the environment which best meets their needs and that this is not always the mainstream school.

Despite the move towards inclusion, one group of young people continue to be excluded. The behaviour of these young people is disruptive and they pose problems for schools. No debate on inclusion can ignore the fact that behaviour is a major issue in relation to inclusion.

POINTS FOR REFLECTION

1 All young people have the right to be included in mainstream schools. Exclusion violates human rights. What are your views in relation to these statements?

2 Most professionals agree with inclusion in principle but consider that there are barriers which need to be overcome if inclusion is to become a reality in practice. What do you think some of these potential barriers are and how might they be addressed?

3 The *Count Us In* report made it clear that one of the major challenges facing schools is to include those who are marginalised because of their disruptive behaviour. What are the particular challenges that this group poses and how should schools respond?

The curriculum and behaviour

> ❝ It is better to approach a solution to disaffection through curricular reform. By developing a rich, varied, stimulating curricula, which involves pupils, whatever their ability, teachers can often afford to reduce the stress on behaviour. ❞
>
> **(Coulby, 1987)**

Defining the curriculum

The curriculum is an evolving entity which must respond to the needs of an ever-changing society. To understand this process of change, one must take account of the moral, social, intellectual, economic and political dimensions. It is within the societal structure that schools operate and are expected to produce young people who are socially and emotionally literate, and who can take on the role of successful learners, confident individuals, responsible citizens and effective communicators (Curriculum for Excellence, 2007). However, as Kelly (2004) strongly stresses, any curriculum development which does not take into account the centrality of the teacher's role is doomed to failure, and over the last decade or so in Scotland, this has proved to be the case.

It is a true saying that you can take a horse to the water but you cannot make it drink. This statement most certainly applies to many teachers who have in the past paid lip service to any curriculum development they have seen as being imposed on them. It cannot, therefore, be assumed that under these circumstances, teachers are willing simply to internalise the received wisdom passed down by those who, to say the least, are not necessarily *au fait* with the realities of school life. Teachers are professionals, and they are happy to internalise new developments if they are given time to stand back and reflect upon them and internalise those elements which support them in their role as educators, and which they see as benefiting their pupils.

As far back as 1971, Richmond used the adjective 'slippery' to describe the curriculum. The intention was to convey how complex it was to reach a consensus on a definition. Taking a narrow perspective, the curriculum can be seen to be synonymous with a set syllabus or scheme of work linked to identifiable subject disciplines. Alternatively, taking the broadest view, the curriculum is wide ranging and embraces the totality of learning experiences and opportunities provided as part of the education process as a whole.

While it is true to say that over the past 30 years this definition of the curriculum has been revised and refined, it cannot simply be implied that all teachers have internalised this more holistic view. However, it is vital that teachers, who are, after all, at the front line and have the ultimate responsibility to deliver an appropriate curriculum accessible to all pupils, are able to answer the question – what is the curriculum?

It is not my intention at this point to delve too deeply into the concept of the curriculum or to explore curricular theory. I do, however, want to focus upon how an ill-defined curriculum can impose barriers to learning for young people who already feel alienated and marginalised. My aim at this point is to demonstrate how a restricted view of the curriculum on the teacher's part has a direct impact on how she/he responds to the needs of all learners and to this more challenging group in particular. The curriculum has the power to alleviate or exacerbate disaffected behaviour.

As I have already indicated the curriculum is complex and it is not easy to sum up what it is in a few words. At the risk of being accused of oversimplification, I would say that in essence, there are two major views. The first is the traditional view described by Bantock (1980) as the combined range of courses of study available to learners in an educational establishment. In contrast, Woods and Orlik (1994) take the wider view that the curriculum cannot be considered simply as formal course of study, but includes the school's ethos, the quality of relationships, the concern for equality of opportunity, and the values exemplified across a curriculum which is organised, managed and taught in a child-centred manner.

I would suggest that it is the latter view which prevails in schools where all learners are equally valued and where teachers appreciate the link between an appropriate curriculum and effective teaching and learning. In addition, they are aware of the importance of making every effort to deliver an inclusive curriculum, which caters for diversity in learning and appreciates the interaction between the curriculum and behaviour

The hidden curriculum

Kelly (2004) examines what the curriculum is and enables the reader to clarify their understanding of the term. He discusses some key ideas under the following headings:

- the formal and informal curriculum
- the planned and received curriculum
- the hidden curriculum.

All of the points he raises are relevant to all learners. I would, however, strongly identify the hidden curriculum as having a major impact on young people whose behaviour can be challenging. To understand and respond to such behaviour, teachers must fully appreciate what is meant by the hidden curriculum and their role in conveying it to the learners in their classrooms. Effective teachers are well aware of how their attitudes, values and expectations can influence and shape young people in an enduring way. The following scenarios serve to illustrate this point.

Scenario 1 – Do as I say not as I do

The Primary 5 teacher constantly emphasises to her pupils that it is very important to apologise when you are in the wrong. When she goes out to the playground to collect her class she hears someone swearing. Derek had been behaving badly that morning and she is annoyed with him so without thinking things through she blames him. He protests but the teacher ignores him. At that point a colleague who saw what happened takes her aside and explains that Derek was not the culprit. The Primary 5 teacher then turns to Derek in front of the whole class and says 'You might not be the culprit this time but your behaviour is still not acceptable and it makes a change that you are not to blame this time'.

Scenario 2 – The bottom set

At the end of second year, secondary school X set their pupils according to attainment. The theory behind this approach is that it puts pupils of similar abilities together and this should enable their needs to be met more effectively. Sheila has learning difficulties, particularly in relation to reading, but until recently she has tried at all times to do her very best. She is placed in the lowest ability set. The majority of teachers in the school refer to this as 'the bottom set', although if asked they would say they do not say this in front of the pupils. It is noticeable that Sheila's behaviour, which has been good, has begun to deteriorate. When she is asked by her guidance teacher about this she says 'What do you expect? I am in the bottom set and everyone knows that's just the same as the stupid class for people who are thick'.

It is through the hidden curriculum that young people learn about authority, bureaucracy, gender differentiation, ability, fairness, equality and rights. A young person will learn about these things only if the teacher is able to model this behaviour. This can be done as part of a structured personal and social development class, but fundamentally these values can also be conveyed via the formal curriculum by a teacher who has internalised and prioritised these values.

It is not possible to understand why some young people misbehave without considering the pupil–teacher relationship. The hidden curriculum plays a significant part in developing a positive valuing relationship. It is not always easy for a teacher to form effective relationships with his/her pupils, especially when the numbers in the class are high, and we must keep in mind that teachers are human and life can be very difficult when faced with disruptive behaviour. Nonetheless, effective teachers know that it is worth taking the time to get to know their pupils and relate to them. It is, in fact, not possible to stand in front of a class of young people day in, day out without conveying how you really feel about them. If a teacher thinks the class is the class from hell she/he never needs to use these words; it will be conveyed all too clearly through the hidden curriculum. In 1986, the Scottish Consultative Committee on the Curriculum (SCCC) produced the *10–14 Report* which highlighted the importance of the hidden curriculum. In their view 'the classroom crackles with subliminal signals – about our moral priorities, our view of society and the individual's place in it ... pupils become adept at reading these daily messages.' The reader may like to consider the subliminal message(s) being conveyed in the following scenarios.

Scenario 3 – Sarcasm, the lowest form of wit

Teacher X meets some colleagues from other schools at an in-service course. They start to talk about their schools and teacher X says that she is delighted that after the summer holidays she is joining the staff of a 'good school'. When talking about her present school she says 'I just can't wait to get out of that hell-hole and teach some normal children'.

Scenario 4 – Stereotyping and self-fulfilling prophecies

Students studying to be teachers are discussing the schools they will be going to for a period of school experience. One student seems pleased and when asked why says 'it has a great reputation and its exam results were the best of all the schools in that authority'. A second student appears to be in despair and responds as follows: 'It's alright for you I am going to school X – it's in a very rough neighbourhood with lots of problem kids from dysfunctional families, I don't know how I am meant to motivate them.' A lecturer who has overheard these conversations asks the students if they have actually been in these schools and they reply that they have not but they have heard about them through the grapevine.

Scenarios 3 and 4 demonstrate the more negative aspects of the hidden curriculum. They make the point that teachers cannot conceal their deep-rooted attitudes and expectations and that it is virtually impossible not to convey these subliminal messages to their pupils.

However, all effective teachers are well aware of the power of the hidden curriculum as a positive force which can be used to motivate and show that all learners are valued equally. As part of their research into effective support systems for young people Hamill and Boyd (2003) interviewed young people to ascertain their views on a range of subjects. The young people were extremely perceptive and demonstrated clearly that they were skilled at identifying teachers who consistently conveyed positive messages via the hidden curriculum. One girl spoke for the majority of her peers when talking about what she described as good teachers:

> Good teachers have a relaxed kind of class, they speak to you as if you are a person and they listen to you. They are like a sort of friend and have a sense of humour but they still teach you and make you work hard. They have a kind of presence and they are calm. It's just something about them that is difficult to put into words.

It is vital, therefore, that teachers are aware of how the hidden curriculum reveals a great deal about how their value systems operate. It influences all young people and it is extended and reinforced by the teacher's behaviour. Young people whose behaviour is challenging can be particularly perceptive, especially in environments which send the message to them that they are less valued. In these circumstances they may choose to reject the norms conveyed to them by the school and to embrace nonconformity.

The chicken or the egg?

A conundrum I have grappled with throughout my career in education revolves around the question, 'do learning difficulties result in challenging behavior or is it the disruptive behaviour which causes difficulties in learning?' As one would expect there is, of course, no straightforward answer and it would be reasonable to conclude that both aspects of this puzzling question are valid.

There are, without doubt, some young people in our schools whose behaviour is very challenging, who experience social and emotional difficulties and could be described as seriously disaffected. In some schools these young people are referred to as 'high tariff' due to the severity of their behavioural difficulties. They often have psychological and mental health issues (Farrell, 1995; Cole *et al.*, 1998).

Hamill and Boyd (2000; 2003) undertook two research projects which considered the nature and range of disruptive behaviour in the secondary school and explored specifically the effectiveness of behaviour support units as an alternative to exclusion. They identified some of the common factors shared by individuals in this high tariff group and these are outlined below:

- excluded from school on innumerable occasions, often fairly early on in the primary school
- causing disruption in the majority of subject classrooms which was seriously affecting the education of their peers
- displaying acting out behaviour which was often threatening, aggressive and anti-social
- restricted emotional and behavioural development due to negative experiences within dysfunctional families
- causing disruption in the community, e.g. vandalism/fighting. Often known to the police
- abusing alcohol and/or drugs
- the young person places little value on education and schooling in particular.

This group of young people is described in the *Count Us In* report (HMIE, 2002) as seriously disaffected. The *Better Behaviour – Better Learning* report (SEED, 2001) also expressed concern about the 'extremely disturbed behaviour exhibited by troubled young people who face major challenges in their lives' (SEED, 2001, p. 11). It is, therefore, very important to acknowledge that even when teachers strive to do their very best, these seriously disaffected young people often present problems which are deep rooted and complex and they often require additional specialist support which in reality is not always forthcoming. Many of these young people face barriers to their learning which often leads to them feeling dissatisfied with the education on offer. These barriers include learning difficulties, inaccessible curriculum and inappropriate teaching, all of which can impact negatively on behaviour.

The research evidence suggests that there is a strong correlation between disruptive behaviour and learning difficulties. Garner and Gains (1996, p. 143) made this point when discussing their findings that too often the heavy emphasis some schools place 'upon the inappropriate or anti-social behaviour of some pupils may deflect from their attendant learning difficulties'. This was borne out by the work of Booth and Coulby (1987), O'Brien (1998) and Olsen and Cooper (2001). In 2000 and 2003 Hamill and Boyd provided further evidence to show this link. They found that, of the young people in one education authority's secondary schools who had all been excluded from school on more than one occasion and were receiving support in Pupil Support Bases, the majority experienced some level of difficulty in learning.

Hamill and Boyd also found that it was the young people themselves in the first instance and their parents who very quickly made the connection between learning difficulties as a potential source of disruptive behaviour.

> I have asked him repeatedly why he acts the clown in class. He says he doesn't know. I think it has a lot to do with trying to take attention away from his problems with reading and writing.
>
> (Parent)

> The teacher told me to do the work but I couldn't. He just said I should be able to do it so I just sat and did nothing. He started to ask me hard questions and I didn't know the answers so I swore under my breath and he threw me out of the class.
>
> (Pupil)

Smith (1992) hits the nail on the head when he argues that the challenge for schools is to find appropriate ways to prevent difficulties in learning becoming translated into challenging behaviour, by creating learning opportunities which result in success rather than leading to feelings of failure, incompetence, inadequacy and inevitably disruption. The key lies in curriculum development which has at its core the principle of valuing every young person.

Producing or reducing disaffection

Two findings emerged strongly from the research undertaken by Hamill and Boyd (2000; 2003). They concluded that in many of the classes observed:

1 There were a small but significant minority of young people whose behaviour was so challenging that they were negatively affecting the learning of their peers.
2 The curriculum was inappropriate and consequently it was a source of both learning and behavioural difficulties.

Over the past few years I have worked with many primary and secondary teachers, and it is interesting to see how they respond to the above findings. It is difficult to find anyone who will not agree wholeheartedly with statement 1 but there is usually a less enthusiastic response to statement 2. The fact is that both statements are valid and although many teachers may agree in principle with statement 2, which focuses on the nature of the curriculum, the vast majority still tend to give much higher priority to statement 1, which is more concerned with the inbuilt individual deficiencies on the pupil's part. This view was consistently expressed by teachers who accept the principle that all children have the right to be educated but object to the amount of time and energy given to a minority of disruptive pupils to the detriment of others in the class who want to learn. It is therefore important for teachers to extend their perceptions in relation to the factors which exacerbate indiscipline, and one very important factor which must be acknowledged is that an inappropriate curriculum can produce challenging behaviour. It is through the curriculum that messages are received about the value and status of individuals.

Unfortunately, some young people internalise the feeling that they are of less value. They feel on the periphery of schools which dismiss their cultures or show little respect for them or their families. Teachers have a responsibility to ensure that they are doing everything they can to put in place a curriculum which is stimulating, flexible, diverse and inclusive. It may be painful for some teachers to accept that some young people may not behave as they should because of what they are taught and the way they are being taught. The mismatch between their additional needs and the delivery of the curriculum is a fundamental issue and should lead schools to reflect carefully upon their own practices rather than simply putting the responsibility on young people. Teaching can be a very stressful occupation and teachers rightly feel at times they are not given the practical support they need. It is therefore important to emphasise that the majority of teachers are happy to accept their professional responsibilities as long as the difficulties they often face are acknowledged in a climate which recognises that they too have legitimate personal and professional needs and human rights.

The work of Glasser (1998) helps to illustrate the importance of a relevant accessible curriculum. He places emphasis on the curriculum being perceived as 'useful' and highlights the fact that young people will never be motivated by a system which views them as passive recipients of an uninspiring curriculum which takes little account of their needs or abilities. Glasser makes the link between what he describes as the futile curriculum and demotivated young people. He says that boredom is the enemy of quality and this will be recognised by teachers who are all too familiar with young people who respond to some tasks with the words 'Miss, this is really boring'. One can dismiss such views out of hand or reflect upon the extent to which they are true. The curriculum must provide learning opportunities which are inherently satisfying for those on the receiving end.

In 1978 the Scottish Education Department (SED) produced the report entitled *The Education of Pupils with Learning Difficulties in Primary and Secondary Schools in Scotland*. It has since proved to be a seminal report, instrumental in helping teachers reassess their views as to why some young people fail to learn. One of the underlying messages was that young people were experiencing difficulties due to 'the fact that they were having to tackle work which is not suitable for them' (p. 23). They went on to say that they believed the proper approach to the problem was through an appropriate and accessible curriculum. At the time of this report I was a Principal Teacher of Remedial Education in a large comprehensive secondary school operating a system of extraction based on the view that learning difficulties resided within individuals and these had to be remedied by removing young people from their peers for remedial education. Like many of my colleagues at that time, I was not prepared simply to accept the received wisdom passed down by SED. They did, of course, provide food for thought but it was only when I was able to apply this wisdom to my own practice that I took on board their recommendations. Over the past twenty years I have become totally convinced that the curriculum can be a source of learning and/or behavioural difficulties. I have selected two scenarios which I hope will provide for the reader concrete examples of the inappropriate curriculum in action.

Scenario 5 – Can't see the wood for the trees

Martin is in Primary 5. He has some difficulties in learning but to date his behaviour has been reasonable. Recently his teacher has begun to notice some signs of low level disruption. The class has been working on a language topic and all pupils have been given the same task. Martin's response to this task is provided on the following page.

salad	seven	robin	melon
petal	given	blanket	lemon
medal	driven	devil	dragon
signal			

All these words have two vowels.
Underline the vowels.
Write the words in a list
in alphabetical order.

Name the pictures.
Write the words.
Underline the vowel sounds.

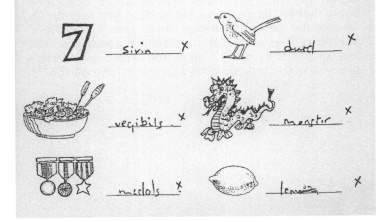

It is clear that Martin has not understood the task. He has not made the connection between naming the pictures and the information provided in the box at the top of the worksheet, although his answers are really quite logical e.g. 'vegibils' and 'monstir'. The response also shows how certain experiences have been taken for granted e.g. Martin cannot recognise salad servers as an indication that the bowl contains salad and he cannot make a distinction between a monster and a dragon.

Scenario 6 – Failure – A vicious circle

Derek is in the third year at secondary school. He has been excluded due to his disruptive behaviour several times and has just returned from one of these exclusions. He arrives late to his geography class and his teacher shows that he is not exactly pleased to see him. Even before Derek has had time to sit down the teacher warns him that he will not be tolerating any bad behaviour. Derek is given the set task and told to get on with it. He stares at it for a few minutes and says he can't do it. His teacher says they have already covered all of this work and he should be able to do it. Derek starts to write. There is a series of diagrams with related questions. Derek's response to the first and the last question are given on the following pages.

Climate Assessment - General

Reference Diagram Q1A : Climate Graph of Tropical Rainforest

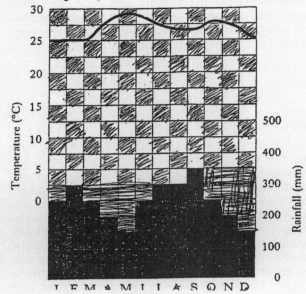

Look at Reference Diagram Q1A.
Describe in detail the climate of the Tropical Rainforest.

This is. _____ Speak ung and I
am bad so dont mess with me
I know I am going to mess up
This ~~test~~ so what this is the story
about. , ?

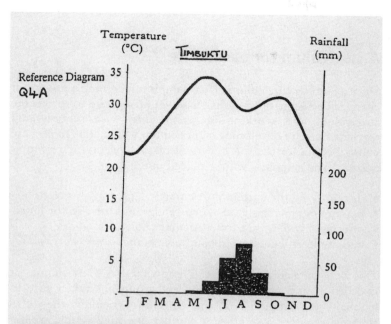

Reference Diagram Q4A

Temperature (°C) / TIMBUKTU / Rainfall (mm)

Look at Reference Diagram Q4A.

Describe the climate of Timbuktu **in detail**.

This is Becoming a Joke so leave me alone please

When the teacher sees Derek's response he is very annoyed and says that he is just a waste of space. Derek gets angry and a heated verbal exchange ensues and he is told to get out of the class.

A curriculum for excellence

Once again the curriculum in Scotland is undergoing a process of change. The Scottish Executive have set up a group to review the curriculum and working in partnership with schools and teachers they are developing a curriculum which aims to prepare young people for the role they will play as twenty-first century citizens. The emphasis will be placed upon:

- de-cluttering the current curriculum
- making more cohesive cross-curricular and inter-sector links
- offering a wider range of curricular choice
- making learning enjoyable and interesting.

This new curricular initiative is known as 'A Curriculum for Excellence' and although the review group has taken care to highlight the strengths of the current curriculum they also acknowledge that a significant number of young people are not attaining their full potential. Young people who are disaffected by school are part of this significant number and they present particular challenges to those responsible for planning and delivering a more innovative curriculum. Collaboration and partnership with schools and teachers underpins the Curriculum for Excellence initiative and professionals in schools are actively encouraged to be flexible and to apply professional judgements in planning programmes and activities to respond to the needs of individual learners. Teachers are expected to be creative and work across and beyond traditional subject boundaries. Curriculum relevance is prioritised and young people should now understand the purpose and value of what they are asked to do. Learning and teaching should relate to their lives now and as future adults.

Thus A Curriculum for Excellence provides schools with an opportunity to devise an alternative, more relevant curriculum for those young people who feel devalued, alienated and marginalised. Some education authorities have already taken up this challenge and they have started to tailor the curriculum, particularly in secondary schools, to cater for the needs of some of the more troubled students. The aim is to provide a more effective balance between the academic, social, personal and vocational dimensions. A wide range of learning opportunities is covered:

- working with FE colleges to extend the curriculum choices such as hairdressing, motor mechanics, and hospitality and catering
- developing enterprise activities
- work experience and community links
- outdoor education
- developing ICT skills
- developing social skills
- careers education and guidance
- attaining relevant academic qualifications.

In this way some forward-thinking schools are striving to provide an inclusive, differentiated, alternative curriculum which satisfies the two prime requirements of the Curriculum for Excellence. It has to reflect the broad aims of education which hold good for all young people, and it has to allow for differences in ability and other characteristics of young people. This is the challenge for schools and they should be enabled to meet this challenge more effectively within the framework being suggested as part of A Curriculum for Excellence. One of the keys to success is to establish a multidisciplinary team which utilises the skills, not only of teachers, but of other professionals such as social workers and community education workers.

As with any new curricular initiative there are flaws which can mar effective progress if not tackled. Great care has to be taken if a school decides to develop an alternative curriculum. All staff have to be actively involved in the curriculum development, see that they are part of the decision-making process and accept ownership of the initiative. There is a danger that it will be viewed by some teachers as taking away responsibility from them for those learners who are seen to be the responsibility of the members of the team who work directly with disaffected young people. The mentality can quickly emerge that these disruptive young people are the responsibility of the teachers who form the core alternative curriculum team. It is all too easy for the alternative curriculum to become something which is different and apart from the mainstream curriculum, rather than a related set of complementary experiences.

If due care is not taken in planning the alternative curriculum it can be seen as vocational and non-academic. To succeed there must also be an emphasis placed upon developing the academic potential of the young people. Creating an alternative curriculum appears to be a positive way forward but schools should proceed with caution. It must be seen as useful and purposeful or it can simply become a second-class curriculum for a second-class colony of pupils who forfeit the right to be part of the wider school community. As Solity (1993) points out, planning and delivering a curriculum which caters for diversity is a complex and skilled process. It challenges the professional competence of teachers, requiring them to find satisfactory outcomes from a range of perspectives.

SUMMARY

Defining the curriculum is not an easy task. It is complex, multifaceted and is responsive to the needs of an ever changing society. If one looks at the dictionary definition, the curriculum is often described as a list of all the courses of study offered by the school. However, this traditional curricular view is now recognised as too simplistic as it does not take enough account of the social and emotional dimensions. The curriculum is now expected to respond to a wide diversity of learner need and must embrace the totality of experiences and learning opportunities provided by the school.

The curriculum has the potential to both alleviate and exacerbate learning and behavioural difficulties. When insufficient care is taken in relation to planning and developing an inclusive and appropriate curriculum, it becomes less accessible, poses barriers to learning, and leads to boredom, frustration and disruption.

There is an important part of the curriculum which is described as hidden and it is via this hidden curriculum that many subliminal messages are conveyed to young people. These messages can impact positively on their lives and indicate to them the extent to which they are valued and respected. In contrast, negative messages emphasise that some young people are seen as being on the periphery of school life. The hidden curriculum sends out strong vibes about the school's and the teacher's value systems.

Another related factor which can easily be overlooked is the link between learning difficulties and behavioural difficulties. When this happens, emphasis is often placed upon the presenting challenging behaviour and less importance is given to the attendant learning difficulties and the barriers they pose for young people. Schools and teachers must develop their awareness of how a mismatch between the curriculum and the learner's needs can produce, rather than reduce, disaffection.

Thus the curriculum is constantly changing and adapting to meet the needs of society. This can be seen from the emphasis now placed on the four capacities of A Curriculum for Excellence. This new curricular initiative aims to make the educational experience for all young people more relevant and meaningful. Schools should now have more scope to deliver an innovative curriculum which helps all young people reach their full potential.

POINTS FOR REFLECTION

1 To understand and respond to the needs of young people whose behaviour is disruptive, professionals must fully appreciate what is meant by the hidden curriculum and their role in conveying subliminal messages to young people. To what extent are professionals aware of this vital element of the curriculum and its impact upon learners?

2 The curriculum has the potential to either reduce or produce disaffection. Do you agree? Is it possible for mainstream schools to develop a curriculum which caters for a diverse range of pupil needs, including, in particular, those whose behaviour is challenging?

3 Some schools are developing an alternative curriculum aimed at meeting more effectively the needs of young people who display troublesome behaviour. In what way(s) is this a sensible approach? Are there pitfalls inherent in such an approach?

6 Better learning – better behaviour

> It seems clear that where appropriate consideration is given to learning and teaching approaches and where the quality of learning and teaching is consistently high, with the appropriate balance of challenge and support enshrined within an atmosphere of high expectations, discipline problems can be reduced significantly.

(SEED, 2001)

Effective learning – the heart of the matter

There are undoubtedly factors which reside within an individual's personal and social development which predispose them towards disruptive behaviour. It is also evident that the home and the community greatly influence behaviour. It can be difficult but schools must do their best to try and exert an influence on these factors and many do so with considerable success. Schools cannot be held responsible for problems which have their source outwith the school, although teachers are often on the receiving end of the resulting behaviour. If, however, teachers take a child-centred view they will see it as part of their role to take a holistic approach to meeting the young person's needs.

Most teachers are committed professionals and strive to create learning climates which address these needs. All too often when the teacher asks for support it is seen as a sign of weakness and this view needs to be challenged. When a teacher is able to prove that they have done their very best to support a young person, then it is a mark of professionalism to ask for support but it may also be difficult to avoid excluding a young person.

Two factors which must be considered before resorting to exclusion are the calibre of teaching on offer and the quality of the learning opportunities planned and delivered. If an individual is to be excluded from a classroom, it seems logical to assume that prior to this decision being taken, everything has been done to ensure that as far as possible there are no barriers within the learning context which are exacerbating the young person's behavioural difficulties. It is the teacher's job to ensure these barriers are removed if they relate to the teaching and learning process.

This is an area in which schools are expected to have a direct responsibility. Hamill and Boyd (2000; 2003) found considerable variation in practice. They found many teachers who could be described as extended professionals and who put in a considerable amount of additional time and effort to be innovative, creative and inspiring. Others could be described as mediocre, and some were restricted professionals who saw issues in black and white and perceived the young people to be to blame. As part of their research Hamill and Boyd shadowed some young people who had been excluded due to their behavioural difficulties. Ann was in S2 and she was one of these young people. The following is the result of a morning's observation.

Observing Ann

Period 1 – Modern Studies and the lesson was about the 'The British Parliament'. The teacher used a set textbook and tried to expand on the issues covered in this text. The readability level of the textbook meant that it was difficult for a few young people with reading difficulties and the language and concepts covered were fairly complex. Several pupils found it difficult and Ann was one of them. The lesson was tedious and boring and little attempt was made to make it interesting or relevant. Everyone sat in rows and had to attempt the same work. Ann asked the teacher what the word 'democracy' meant and he did his best to explain. A boy nearby called Ann 'thick' under his breath. Ann retaliated with a swear word and a slanging match ensued. The teacher eventually put both pupils outside the room and said he was reporting them to the Principal Teacher.

Period 2 and 3 – English. Ann's teacher made a point of asking her about her father, who was not very well. The class worked in groups. Ann seemed happy in this class and with a bit of encouragement from the teacher entered into the discussion about things that make you frightened. The teacher used an excellent video clip and photographs to stimulate discussion. She developed a word bank and gave everyone a plan to assist them writing a scary story. When Ann got stuck the teacher helped her talk through her ideas one to one and gave her and some others a slightly modified plan. Ann produced a piece of writing which was shorter and less detailed than some of her friends but it showed that she had done her best. At the end of the session the teacher selected several stories, including Ann's, which she read to the class. She said the pupils could word process their work next time. She praised everyone for their efforts and wrote, 'A very scary story. You used some good words to describe how you felt – Well done.' on Ann's jotter.

Period 4 – Maths. The teacher started to shout at the class as soon as they arrived. She seemed to anticipate difficulties but at this point the class appeared to be quite well behaved. A boy said he had lost his pencil and the teacher started a long lecture about being prepared. The class was getting restless. The lesson on the addition of fractions began and the class was given some practical activities to do. A few young people said they had done this before and the teacher said the extra practice would do them good. Some young people, including Ann, obviously did not understand what was expected of them and they were quickly off task discussing a TV programme. The teacher intervened and told them if they did not get on with the task they would do it for homework. Ann said she needed help and the teacher gave her a photocopied page of easier sums taken from a workbook. Ann looked puzzled and a bit embarrassed.

It is clear that the quality of learning and teaching Ann is experiencing is varied. If one is to understand fully why her behaviour can be challenging, it is important to consider her personal, social and emotional difficulties and the impact of her home life. However, it is also vital to look closely at the process of learning and teaching. It is particularly interesting to reflect on some of the issues emerging from observing Ann.

- Who apart from visiting researchers would have this overview of Ann's experiences?
- What mechanisms exist in the school for excellent teachers to share their good practice?
- What support is available for less effective teachers?
- To what extent does the shape of the school day contribute to the learning and behaviour of some young people?

It is obvious that Ann's English teacher is most effective in relation to providing for her the best learning experience. She understands that differentiation is a vital prerequisite for effective teaching, learning and behaviour. This teacher demonstrates in practice the view expressed by Hamill and Clark (2005, p. 105) who said that 'the aim of differentiation is to maximise opportunity for all learners and aid access to an appropriate curriculum'. This English teacher adapted the way the work was set in order to meet the range of abilities within her class. She shows some evidence that she is trying to implement in practice the five types of differentiation highlighted by Stradling and Saunders (1993). Differentiation by:

- task – learners cover the same content at different levels
- outcome – a similar task is set for all learners but flexibility is built in so that individuals can progress at their own level
- pace – the same content is covered at the same level but at a different rate
- dialogue – the teacher discusses the task with the learner to ensure that it is meeting their needs
- learning activity – tackling the same task at the same level but in a different way.

These types of differentiation do not have to apply to all of the learning opportunities planned and delivered by the teacher. They are, in fact, complementary and the particular focus can vary depending on the task to be undertaken.

Differentiation is at the core of the teaching/learning process. It encourages teachers to take on board their responsibility to ensure that there is a vital link between successful learning and positive behaviour. The *Better Behaviour – Better Learning* report (SEED, 2001) does, without doubt, make this connection. However, I would suggest that the title of the report does not convey this as effectively as it might. Better learning is at the heart of the matter and is the prerequisite for better behaviour.

Climates for learning

In the previous chapter I argued that professionals must adopt a wider perspective when thinking about the question 'what is the curriculum?' I concluded that the curriculum is, in the last analysis, a composite of everything that happens in a school. It is not just about the planned learning opportunities but also the context in which they are delivered, and this is usually within the classroom. In short, it is not just what teachers do that is important, it is the way that they do it. One of the crucial ways of doing it is to ensure the climate in the classroom is conducive to effective learning. Productive learning environments have been the subject of several studies (Freiberg and Stein, 1999; Muijs and Reynolds, 2001). These writers identify some basic elements which are characteristic of positive learning environments. These include the teacher–pupil relationship, the mood or atmosphere in the classroom, the focus on effective learning, an inclusive curriculum and the physical environment. It is also within this kind of climate that challenging behaviour becomes less problematic.

Rutter *et al.* (1979) presented sound evidence which demonstrated that the crucial factor was the ethos conveyed within schools and classrooms. The prevailing ethos gives the school and classroom its distinctive characteristics. It is the means by which individuals demonstrate their system of values, and these individual actions may combine to create a particular set of attitudes, values and behaviours which can become the distinctive features of the school as a whole. Through their leadership and vision, the senior management in a school play a very significant part in ensuring the ethos is positive. However, on a day-to-day basis the people whom young people come into direct contact with are teachers and to an appreciable extent the behaviour and attitudes of these young people are influenced by their interactions with teachers.

McLean (1991) worked with schools and teachers to produce some excellent staff development resources designed to help schools become more effective in the promotion of positive behaviour. The concept of ethos permeated these resources and one activity in particular aimed to help teachers ascertain the ethos factor in relation to their classrooms. Teachers were asked to rate their own ethos by highlighting ten words from the following list which they thought best described their classroom climate.

Ethos factor

friendly chaotic calm open hostile lively caring fair strict stressed tolerant impersonal depressing optimistic supportive cynical purposeful confident flexible insular elitist rigid innovative trusting orderly insensitive nurturing authoritarian divisive welcoming democratic child-centred repressive respectful controlling enthusiastic embattled honest confused organised sympathetic controlling sarcastic genuine

---

Some words are negative and some positive. By looking at the words the teacher can rate her/his ethos on a scale of minus 10 to plus 10. It is, of course, best if the ethos is actually rated by the learners and if a teacher wants a true indication of ethos he/she may wish to try out this activity with the pupils who are on the receiving end.

The reflective professional needs to occasionally stand back and reflect upon his/her practice. For example it is not enough for a teacher to simply say that his/her ethos is positive without presenting evidence of the practice which supports this view. I have devised the following checklist to provide a context for this reflective process.

Reflecting on the Learning/Teaching Process
I am able to admit errors/lack of experience – I was wrong.
I promote learning as a shared/co-operative experience.
I appreciate that all learners have strengths and capitalise on these.
I accept that experiencing difficulty is a natural part of the learning process.
Praise and encouragement is a vital part of my teaching.
I always try to anticipate potential problems.
I listen to my learners and empathise with them.
I capitalise upon the interests of my learners.
I am an effective learner and model this to my pupils.
I am aware of the power of the hidden curriculum.
I enhance self-esteem.
I appreciate the relationship between the curriculum and behaviour.
I provide opportunities for learners to express difficulties and discuss problems.
I do not dominate the learning process.
I utilise a wide range of styles, techniques and strategies.
I do not make learners feel stupid or inadequate.
I do not make assumptions regarding the knowledge or experiences of my learners.
I am patient and try not to get exasperated with my learners.
I learn from my pupils and do not present the image of the all-knowing expert.
I am approachable.
I never see questioning as threatening.
I treat everyone fairly and equally.
I am honest in my dealings with pupils.
My pupils know that I like them.

We often ask our pupils to be all they can be and it is important that teachers are able to consider their own practice and to be all they can be. Checklists like the one on the previous page provide examples of good practice and teachers may find them helpful. However, by their nature they are limited and most teachers would be able to think of innumerable other qualities effective professionals should possess. The bottom line for the teacher is that they should realise the significance they play in creating positive learning climates and how their behaviour influences their learners.

Self-fulfilling prophecies — the labelling process

As far back as 1968 Rosenthal and Jacobsen demonstrated the connection between the teacher's expectations of their pupils and their subsequent academic success or lack of it. They produced convincing evidence to support their views suggesting that when teacher's attitudes and expectations were negative they resulted in stereotyping some pupils as low achievers. Thus a vicious circle developed fuelling the self-fulfilling prophecy whereby learners internalised these negative stereotypical images, saw themselves as failures and behaved accordingly. A considerable body of research evidence over the past 50 years has confirmed the conclusions of Rosenthal and Jacobsen and extended their findings to include behaviour.

McNamara and Moreton (2001) and Rogers (2004) provide evidence that there is a tendency for some teachers to make predictions about the type of behaviour they expect, and this creates the stereotypical view of the bad pupil as opposed to focusing upon the inappropriate behaviour. Hamill and Boyd (2000; 2003) found that a recurring theme which arose when interviewing young people who displayed disruptive behaviour was their view that once they had what they called 'a reputation', it appeared almost impossible for them to break out of the self-fulfilling cycle.

Many schools group young people according to ability. This form of organisation is, of course, put in place for what these schools perceive to be sound reasons. Harlen and Malcolm (1997) outline some of these reasons and indicate that the approaches are intended to enable pupils to make progress in line with their ability and assist teachers in their efforts to meet the needs of the group as a whole. Whereas this is the theory underpinning streaming and setting, in practice, Hamill and Boyd (2000) found evidence that for those who find themselves in the lower ability bands, there is the very real danger of being seen as second-class pupils. This view is supported by Kyriacou (1998, p. 42) when he says that often less able pupils get 'caught up in a vicious circle of lowered teacher expectations'.

The young people in these groups are often referred to as in the 'bottom set' and they quickly learn via the hidden curriculum that they are perceived to be at the end of the pecking order. It is quite common to hear teachers say that young people who have behavioural difficulties negatively impact on the rights of their peers. Hamill and Boyd found that in many schools which used setting, the so-called bottom group did not vary from subject to subject. This group was composed of the same learners who had learning and behavioural difficulties which affected their learning in all subject areas. In reality the young people whose rights were most directly affected were the more vulnerable young people who did not misbehave but had learning difficulties. The label 'bottom set' had a major impact on those who were placed there and they often responded to the expectations placed on them by developing a ghetto mentality that was in conflict with the overall school culture, which was seen to be rejecting them.

As mentioned earlier, reputations once acquired are very difficult to discard. The process of labelling is still alive and well in many schools and it can sour the atmosphere in any classroom. I discussed this topic recently with a group of teachers who signed up for a series of continuing professional development sessions I was delivering. I asked them to think about and list the labels which were most often heard in schools. Some of these labels were recognised as being positive e.g. gifted, confident, skilled, diligent, enthusiastic and well behaved, and some others were more negative e.g. nuisance, daydreamer, disinterested, aggressive, hostile, stupid, slow, disturbed. It was clear that when the teachers were asked to think specifically about labels applied to the young people whose behaviour was considered most disruptive, the labels identified emphasised very strongly a sense of cynicism and rejection e.g. waste of space, thug, hooligan, delinquent, yob, lout. Labelling is part and parcel of human life and it is not difficult to see that we live in a society where labelling is rife. Teachers are part of this society and are only human. Their job is stressful and one can to a certain extent understand why they use labels in this way.

The labels used in schools reveal a great deal about the extent to which the school can be described as inclusive. A school is only as inclusive as the professionals who work there and the labels these professionals use tell us a great deal about their values, attitudes and expectations. Teachers have to accept that some labels are offensive and using them is unprofessional. At the same time it must be acknowledged that labelling is an inevitable process and is essential for teachers' understanding of their pupils. It is, however, possible to reduce the negative effect of the labelling process.

1 Avoid drawing hasty conclusions based upon limited evidence.
2 Avoid the sibling syndrome. (You are just like your brother.)
3 Develop your own informed opinions. Don't be influenced by the staffroom cynics.
4 Focus on the behaviour as the problem not the pupil. (He is a bad boy.)
5 Be optimistic – acknowledge signs of better behaviour.
6 Try to put past difficult experiences behind you.
7 Try not to personalise things. (They are all against me.)
8 Look for the strengths. Every human being has them.

This list will simply reaffirm in the majority of teachers what they already do. It will also reinforce within them that by internalising the above approaches, they are demonstrating that they are first and foremost child-centred.

Self-esteem – a fundamental concept

Carlock (1998, p. 3) says that 'simply stated, self-esteem is the way you feel about yourself'. She sees self-esteem in terms of a continuum running from high to low. Every human being wants to feel good about themselves and an individual's self-esteem is a measure of the extent to which they are able to achieve this feelgood factor. Lawrence (1996) makes it clear that the concept of self-esteem is complex. He discusses the self-image (what a person is) and the ideal self (what a person would like to be). For him, self-esteem is the discrepancy between the self-image and the ideal self. This discrepancy is a normal human phenomenon and it is only when it leads to feelings of anxiety and stress that it becomes a problem. High self-esteem is linked to success, happiness, confidence and acceptance. Low self-esteem results in feelings of failure, inadequacy, depression and hopelessness.

Many of the young people in our schools who display disturbed behaviour have low self-esteem. Consequently, they have great difficulty in developing social competence, in adjusting to social contexts, forming relationships, and in learning to follow normal and accepted patterns of behaviour. In addition, their interpersonal skills are restricted and they often have difficulty empathising with others. It can be difficult for the teacher who has to deal with disruptive behaviour to accept the fact that these young people are often very vulnerable and deeply unhappy. On the surface they may convey a sense of bravado, but this can hide serious emotional difficulties. They demand a great deal of a teacher's emotional energy and this can be very draining.

Lawrence (1996) also makes the case that all effective professionals are aware of the effect of self-esteem on behaviour, but some may be better at intuitively enhancing the young person's self-esteem than others. Regardless of how skilled an individual is in this area it is always worthwhile refreshing ourselves in relation to how self-esteem is shaped and influenced. Young people constantly receive messages about their worth as individuals from the significant adults they interact with. Parents are obviously the most significant individuals, but teachers are also highly significant and may take on a vital role in the lives of some young people who come from dysfunctional family backgrounds and have not benefited from a stable nurturing environment.

All teachers have the power to either enhance or damage self-esteem. They can do so as a result of making a conscious decision or they may impart attitudes and expectations subconsciously. It is through experiences in schools and in classrooms in particular that young people form their self-image. This feedback process can be deliberate and planned but more often it is subtle and less obvious. It is in this way that a young person internalises certain beliefs about themselves as people i.e. able/less able, popular/unpopular, included/excluded, assertive/aggressive, calm/anxious. In the same way, they come to realise that there are ideal characteristics which are valued and promoted in schools and these are less easy to acquire for some young people e.g. being clever, being polite, being competitive, being in control and being co-operative.

Leaman (2005) identifies fear as a common element which is highly prevalent in young people whose self-esteem is low. She says that this fear manifests itself in the following ways:

- fear of losing
- fear of not being liked
- fear of not being noticed
- fear of not being accepted
- fear of losing control or of others taking control
- fear of violence
- fear of the unpredictable
- fear of change
- fear of being weak.

I mentioned earlier that many teachers appear to be quite intuitive in the way they enhance self-esteem. In a sense, they respond automatically in a way which reveals their awareness of the vital importance of trying to develop a caring relationship with their pupils. I have experienced this many times in schools and the following scenarios provide examples from my own experience of two excellent teachers enhancing self-esteem.

Scenario 1

I was visiting a primary classroom. I had never met the teacher before. As I entered the classroom there was a hum of purposeful activity as the children worked on various activities. A little toy telephone on the teacher's desk rang and a light flashed. (I had not seen the teacher press a button on the telephone.) She answered the phone telling me it was the head teacher calling and asked if I wished to speak to her. It was obviously a bit of fun and the young people knew this. They looked at me for my reaction and I had to think on my feet. I spoke into the telephone telling the head teacher of my excellent first impressions of the class and how much I was looking forward to spending time with them. The teacher went over and spoke to a boy who came over to me holding his jotter. It had a page of sums, all correct. I asked him his name and informed the (imaginary) head teacher that his work was excellent. He beamed with pleasure and went back to his seat. I said good bye to the headteacher and put the telephone down. I had only been in the room for a few minutes and the teacher had provided opportunities for me to enhance the self-esteem of the whole class and one boy in particular.

Scenario 2

I had been shadowing pupil X for one day in a secondary school. She was a very introverted girl aged thirteen who appeared isolated and withdrawn. She hardly spoke to anyone and tried to merge into the background as much as possible. In most classes she was allowed to do so and it was difficult to see what she was learning if anything.

The day passed in an uneventful way until I arrived late in the afternoon at the science class. The probationer teacher gathered the class around her and started to discuss Marie Curie and radiation. She stopped and asked where pupil X was. It transpired that once again she was hiding at the back of the group. The teacher went round and guided her to the front. She reminded pupil X about the fact she had informed her the previous week about the forthcoming visit to the hospital for an X-ray. The pupil became quite animated and told the class quite eloquently all about her experience. She said she had a copy of her X-ray at home and the teacher asked her to bring it in next time. The teacher asked the class to give pupil X a round of applause for her contribution. Pupil X smiled shyly but appeared to be very happy.

It is in the minutiae of classroom life that we see innumerable examples of excellent teachers at work. Many teachers will recognise something of themselves in these scenarios and they should be commended for their efforts. Teachers also need to have their own self-esteem enhanced, but this often depends on the ability of the senior management team to recognise and praise good classroom practice. It goes almost without saying that if the teacher's self-esteem is low it will be extremely difficult for them to enhance the esteem of their pupils.

SUMMARY

In 2001, the Discipline Task Group wrote the report *Better Behaviour – Better Learning*. This report strongly linked behaviour and learning. However, the title placed the focus upon the learning process being more effective if behaviour was more positive. In this chapter, I have highlighted the need to start with effective teaching and learning as opposed to making behaviour the prime focus of attention. Schools and teachers have a responsibility to create a climate for learning conducive to better behaviour and this must be their starting point.

Careful attention must be paid to the ethos conveyed and its impact upon learners. In some schools, negative labelling still permeates the system and conveys to pupils their sense of worth. It is easy to label some young people negatively and there is a danger that by doing so one simply perpetuates a self-fulfilling prophecy. This is still too often the case for those whose behaviour is deemed to be disruptive. The labels used in schools tell us a great deal about the extent to which the culture could be described as inclusive.

Although it may not always be immediately obvious, many young people with challenging behaviour also experience low self-esteem. Teachers have it in their power to both enhance and damage self-esteem. This concept is fundamental to effective learning, and inspirational teachers are well aware of the need to help young people develop more positive self-esteem.

Schools and teachers who want to promote better behaviour should look first and foremost at the learning opportunities they provide. They must fully appreciate that positive behaviour cannot evolve unless the teaching and learning foundations on which it is built are sound.

POINTS FOR REFLECTION

1. One factor which must be considered before resorting to exclusion is the calibre of teaching on offer and the quality of the learning opportunities planned and delivered. This ultimately is the teacher's responsibility. There is a strong correlation between better learning and better behaviour. To what extent do you agree?

2. The prevailing ethos gives the school and classroom its distinctive characteristics. It is the vehicle whereby professionals demonstrate their value systems and it strongly influences how young people are perceived. It underpins all classroom interactions and impacts directly upon the learning climate. Think about your own work context and reflect upon the prevailing ethos and the evidence you might present to support your viewpoint.

3. Research has demonstrated that teacher expectations can lead to self-fulfilling prophecies and young people often respond to the predictions made about them. This is particularly a matter of concern when the expectations are negative and the young person can easily become trapped within a vicious circle. To what extent is this an issue in schools today? In what ways might negative teacher expectations in relation to a young person's behaviour result in further indiscipline?

7 Managing and promoting positive behaviour

' Everyone who remembers his own educational
experience remembers teachers, not methods
and techniques. '

Sydney Hook

Looking for answers

Over the past twenty years I have planned and delivered many
continuing development courses on behaviour management for
teachers and other professionals. When teachers are asked why
they have chosen to attend courses like this, a common response
is that they are looking for answers to problems relating to the
pupil indiscipline they encounter in classrooms. This is, of
course, understandable, and these individuals are to be
commended for taking the initiative and undertaking courses
which enhance their professional development.

A crucial point which I have made elsewhere in this book is
the fact that in relation to meeting the challenges posed by young
people whose behaviour can be disruptive, there are no quick
fixes or easy solutions. We must be very wary, however, about
making the assumption that there are no solutions. There are, in
fact, a wide range of behaviour management strategies which
can be utilised and result in improved behaviour. Many
publications available on the market today focus on tips and
techniques which can help teachers manage behaviour. It cannot,
however, be automatically assumed that all teachers are equally
able to implement this advice. I am in no way attempting to
apportion blame to teachers. My aim is simply to state clearly
that, in any classroom, the teacher is the key player and just as
young people display a wide range of behaviours so, too, do
teachers. It is not possible, therefore, to consider behaviour

management strategies without reflecting upon what it is about effective teachers which enables them to make the strategies work.

The teacher is the key

It is really only those who work in schools who can appreciate how challenging and demanding teaching is. Too many members of the general public perceive teaching as a job anyone can do and this perception is fundamentally flawed. It is based on limited information and lack of insight into the crucial role teachers play in shaping the lives of young people. Effective teachers are skilled at identifying and meeting the needs of young people and their efforts have a powerful effect on the future of those they teach. Teaching is an art, it is highly skilled, it can be stressful and it is definitely not for the faint-hearted. This is particularly true when faced with young people whose behaviour is disruptive. However, although most teachers face this challenge, some are meeting it more effectively than others.

Those teachers who are able to translate the theory underpinning behaviour management into classroom practice show evidence of personal and professional reflection. They understand that behaviour is first and foremost a relationship issue and in addition to focusing upon pupil behaviour, the teacher must be able to put his/her own behaviour under the microscope. The key individual in any classroom is the teacher, who has the power to influence significantly the lives of those they teach. William Arthur Ward, one of America's most quoted writers and motivational speakers, made this point concisely when he said that the mediocre teacher tells, the good teacher explains, the superior teacher demonstrates and the great teacher inspires.

I have asked many teachers which of the above descriptions they would wish to apply to themselves and it will of course come as no surprise to discover that the overwhelming response is the desire to be inspirational. It must be acknowledged that we are all human and it is not easy to attain this target. What is important is that teachers constantly strive to become inspirational and reject mediocrity at all levels.

All young people deserve to have this kind of child-centred teacher and this includes those who are disaffected, less motivated, and find learning difficult. I would suggest that it is these young people who are in most need of inspirational teachers. In order to illustrate this point I would suggest the reader considers the following task.

Think of a young person whom you love and care for very much (i.e. daughter, nephew, brother, grandson). Their teacher has been offered a one-year secondment and a replacement teacher is to be appointed. You are asked to be a member of the interview panel. What are the characteristics you would look for?

This is an activity I have carried out with many teachers from across all educational sectors and it is interesting to note consistently, that those who respond prioritise the teacher's interpersonal and social skills and ability to create positive learning environments. Characteristics relating to subject knowledge, classroom organisation, methodology, planning and curriculum development are identified as important. However, the characteristics which are rated most highly are friendliness, approachability, being sympathetic, caring, having a sense of humour and being respectful.

It is interesting to note that in his report to the DES on teacher effectiveness, McBer (2000) confirms, on the basis of his research, that the effective teacher is able to model the behaviours they expect from their learners. Thus teachers who require young people to be co-operative, respectful, open, honest, sincere, motivated and considerate must demonstrate in their actions that they have themselves internalised these behaviours. On the initial page of his report McBer outlines the pupils' view of the characteristics of a good teacher as follows:

A good teacher

- is kind
- is generous
- listens to you

- encourages you
- has faith in you
- keeps confidences
- likes teaching children
- likes teaching their subject
- takes time to explain things
- helps you when you are stuck
- tells you how you are doing
- allows you to have your say
- doesn't give up on you
- cares for your opinion
- makes you feel clever
- treats people equally
- stands up for you
- makes allowances
- tells the truth
- is forgiving.

(McBer, 2000)

This may be a tall order, but it does provide a sound framework within which teachers can audit their own practice. The above checklist should be the starting point for all teachers, as it is the teachers who are able to show evidence of these qualities in their practice who will be most effective in implementing a wide range of behaviour management strategies.

Leadership matters

To be effective, teachers need to work in environments where their talents are recognised and where, like the pupils, they are able to thrive. If we want teachers to be inspirational then it is vital that they are part of a team led by inspirational leaders who share the same educational vision. A fundamental aspect of this teamwork is the quality of leadership which prevails in the school. The senior management team play a crucial part in creating the conditions within which every individual in the school feels valued and included. They must model the practice they expect from the staff. It is a case of do what I do not what I say.

Rutter *et al.* (1979) concluded that the hallmark of an effective school was based primarily upon how it functioned as a social institution. This view has been reinforced by research into school effectiveness over the past twenty years (Mortimore *et al.*, 1988; Ainscow, 1991; Scheerens, 1997). All of the crucial factors which schools need to address in their journey towards effectiveness are examined by MacBeath and Mortimore (2001) in the book *Improving School Effectiveness*. One recurring factor is the quality of leadership skills evident within the senior management team and, in particular, the headteacher. If teachers are to find ways of reaching out to alienated young people, they need to be in schools where the senior management team listen to them and are able to bring out the best in them in a way which is nurturing and supportive. In short, teachers also have needs and aspirations and these have to be met if they in turn are to work effectively with young people. Olsen and Cooper (2001, p. 69) describe the differing atmospheres which prevail in schools and their effect upon staff behaviour. In some schools the atmosphere:

> is positive and enriching, imbuing staff and students with a sense of well-being, optimism and confidence. In other schools the atmosphere is toxic, giving rise to a sense of demoralisation, depression and hostility.

The role of the headteacher and his/her senior management team is two dimensional and they are expected to be both managers and leaders. Bush and Middlewood (2005) recognise that effective management and visionary leadership are important. They refer to the work of Bolam (1999) who makes a clear distinction between management and leadership. Management is defined as an executive function relating to the implementation of policy. On the other hand, leadership is much more about shaping the destiny of the school, formulating policies through collaboration and positively transforming systems and establishing a 'can do' solution-focused philosophy.

Harris (2002) undertook research into the nature of school leadership and provides some valuable insights into the features which show evidence of successful leadership. On the following page are the five features identified by Harris, as presented in

Bush and Middlewood (2005). In each case I have tried to expand slightly on how the feature translates into practice.

- Vision and values – The ability to internalise a set of core values and convey them to others. The focus is upon putting people at the centre and giving high priority to developing interpersonal skills.
- Distributive leadership – A shift away from an authoritarian, dictatorial style to one which emphasises democratic principles, teamwork and the sharing of roles and responsibilities.
- Investment in continuing professional development – Actively listening to what staff perceive to be their development needs and jointly creating opportunities to meet these needs in a supportive manner.
- Relationships – The development of relationships is seen to provide the foundations for effective practice. Emphasis is placed upon people as opposed to systems and all staff are encouraged to develop their potential.
- Community building – Awareness that schools are part of the wider community and effective leaders play a significant role in relation to capitalising on the community as a vital learning environment.

Effective leaders lead by example and they show through their behaviour that they can walk the walk as well as talk the talk. This is very important for teachers, who will be encouraged to follow their leader and for young people who see at first hand adults who are appropriate behavioural models. This provides the bedrock upon which consistent whole-school approaches are developed in relation to teaching, learning and behaviour.

Indiscipline is a major barrier to effective teaching and learning. It is also a significant factor in relation to teacher stress. Regardless how effective the teacher is, she/he needs to feel that they are supported. As Rogers (2000) indicates, teachers need to feel secure about the policies and procedures which provide a sound, well understood, whole-school approach to behaviour management. It is important to point out that whereas a whole-school approach is to be commended, there is a danger that it can create robotic teachers who interpret the advice given literally. A policy which does not allow an element of professional flexibility and does not encourage teachers to use their own initiative is doomed to failure. A policy is only as good as the teacher who implements it in practice. Policy making can be complex and creating policies which staff feel they have ownership of is not easy. The following points need to be kept in mind at all times.

1   The need to reject a macho 'right to manage' mentality based upon a top-down management model.
2   Staff will only be committed to the goals of an organisation if they play an active part in their formulation.
3   Success depends upon building on the strengths of staff and ensuring a sense of collaboration permeates the process.
4   The questioning of structures and practices which may have gone unquestioned for many years must be part of the process.
5   An open approach to decision-making is to be encouraged but the management team should work with staff to lay down clear parameters at the outset.
6   Staff must understand the distinction between corporate decision-making and corporate management.
7   An element of conflict is an inevitable part of the overall process and the views of those who differ from the majority must be aired.
8   The forum for discussion should acknowledge that disagreement is acceptable and staff should not feel personally or professionally threatened.
9   Time is of the essence and must be used productively.
10 A system of monitoring, reviewing and evaluating policies should be built in at the planning stage.

The importance of good leadership in schools cannot be overestimated. Leaders have the ultimate responsibility to communicate to teachers, parents and pupils appropriate values, positive ethos and the vision and aspirations for all. Thus they create a culture for positive behaviour which provides the cornerstone for managing behaviour at all levels.

The teacher's management style

It is not easy to comprehend fully why human beings behave in particular ways. The underlying reasons which affect behaviour are more often than not complicated, and there is rarely a straightforward or obvious way of explaining behaviour, particularly behaviour which is challenging. Essentially, human behaviour is a complex phenomenon and any one individual can, in the course of one day, move almost seamlessly from one behaviour to another e.g. supportive, assertive, caring, considerate, withdrawn, polite, cruel, lazy and insolent.

The process of teaching and learning depends on the quality of human interaction between the teacher and the learner. This process must be built upon mutual trust, respect, honesty, equality and above all, the creation of a climate where individuals feel valued. Some teachers mistakenly feel that it is their job to distance themselves from their pupils and to control behaviour. The majority hopefully accept that effective learning rarely results from control and that their role is to shape and influence behaviour and this can only occur if the teacher is able to connect with and establish a link to the pupil. It is virtually impossible to influence another person's behaviour without establishing a positive relationship with him/her.

Basically, teachers have to be skilled at managing behaviour and this means utilising a range of strategies designed to promote acceptable behaviour. As I have previously indicated, these strategies are only as good as the teacher who tries to make them work. In the hands of one teacher they fall flat whereas another consistently applies them successfully. One factor which must be very carefully considered is the management style teachers use. Hook and Vass (2004) have published a very useful pocketbook which covers a range of tips, tools and techniques aimed at helping teachers become more skilled in behaviour management. They place considerable importance upon the need for teachers to reflect carefully on the management style they adopt. Three styles dominate and I think it would be helpful at this point for me to describe these briefly.

Authoritarian

A tight rein must be kept on children at all times. The teacher dominates proceedings, is always in control and deserves automatic respect. Every pupil must be treated the same and little account is taken of differences between pupils or their diversity as learners. Teaching is perceived in terms of a battle where the teacher always wins. This style emphasises punishment and threat, and high priority is placed upon passing on problems to others who are seen as being responsible for sorting the pupil out. The learning climate is usually fairly stressed and there is limited evidence of innovative, creative practice. The deficit model is alive and well and the child-centred approach is not given much priority.

Nurturing

Children are ultimately good and this goodness has to be nourished in an atmosphere of warmth and affection. Friendliness is very important and if the teacher is nice to them the pupils will automatically respond with kindness and they will like her/him. Learning and teaching is fundamentally a democratic process based upon negotiation and mutual respect. We should appeal to the pupil's better nature, reason with them and treat them as equals and politely request that they should behave. In such a climate pupils can feel anxious, unsure and vulnerable and this can result in confusion, disorder and rebellion.

Balanced

Pupils are involved in the decision-making process but recognise that ultimately the teacher is in the driving seat. She/he has the final say and is in command. Indiscipline is acknowledged as a natural part of school life and not something to get too stressed about. The pupils inherently know that the teacher will sort out the problems in an appropriate manner. They trust him/her and look to the teacher for leadership. All pupils are seen to have strengths, and caring means being able to say no and meaning it. The climate is characterised by a culture of appropriate praise, rewards and ensuring pupils learn to take responsibility for their behaviour. The teacher condemns the behaviour not the pupil and maintains the child's dignity at all cost.

It is clear that the management style advocated as most effective is the one which takes a balanced approach where the teacher sets the boundaries, ensures pupils understand that behaviour is based on their response to the choices presented to them and that there are always consequences linked to these choices. It must also be recognised that effective managers of behaviour can identify with aspects of all three styles and are consistently utilising elements of each style depending on the circumstances which prevail. It is the predominant style which counts and it is this style which will impact upon the classroom atmosphere and provides the example for pupils to follow. It is the teacher's underlying educational philosophy which determines their management style and influences their ultimate ability to make behaviour management strategies a reality.

Behaviour management

There are many books on the market which provide excellent practical advice in relation to effective behavioural management. Emmett (2004), Hook and Vass (2004), Rogers (2004) and Leaman (2005) all provide guidance for teachers which is relevant and strongly rooted in the classroom. These authors address the main issues realistically and their guidance is accessible to the busy practitioner.

It is not my intention to revisit the ideas already well presented by these writers. What I do aim to do in this concluding section is provide two self-reflective tasks which an individual may wish to use as part of his/her ongoing continuing professional development. They may also prove useful as workshop activities for schools planning and delivering in-school continuing professional development sessions in relation to challenging behaviour. The two themes addressed are consistency of approach and behavioural support strategies.

Theme 1 – consistency of approach

In any school, it is important that the staff are consistent in the way they work with pupils. Young people need to know what is expected of them and, in particular, the nature and range of behaviour which is acceptable and unacceptable. This consistency of approach is usually enshrined within a whole-school policy which provides a set of guidelines for all staff. Traditionally in schools, these policies were created and handed down by senior managers who often adopted a rigid top-down model of management.

One would not expect to see such approaches nowadays in schools and, although we still have managers who simply pay lip service to a more democratic model, most leaders in school now try to ensure staff have ownership of the policies they are expected to implement. In order to firmly establish a level of consistency of approach across the school, the senior management team must ensure that policies are seen to emerge from the grass roots, and this implies that all staff will have an opportunity to have their say. The initial fundamental question is to consider to what extent all staff share an understanding of what constitutes challenging behaviour. It is only on the basis of a full and frank whole-school discussion that this can be established. The following workshop might provide an initial starting point.

CPD Task 1 – Sharing perspectives

All of the behaviours listed are of concern to some extent. However, some behaviours may be of more or less concern than others. Think about each of the behaviours and allocate a rating of 1, 2 or 3 (1 = of least concern, 3 = of most concern) depending upon your own personal/professional viewpoint. There is no right or wrong answer and all views/responses are equally valid.

The aim of this task is to:

1 Explore the extent to which staff share an understanding of what constitutes unacceptable behaviour.
2 Provide an opportunity for staff to discuss the need for a consistent whole-school approach.
3 Demonstrate the need for a behaviour policy which provides guidance to staff but allows individuals to use their professional judgement depending on the prevailing circumstances.

The overall purpose is to create a forum for interactive professional discussion. It is vital that all views are aired and all viewpoints must be given equal value. The prime function of this activity is to help staff see that it is not easy to develop policies which embrace all views and that an element of compromise will be necessary if a consensus is to be achieved.

Example			
Eating in class/chewing gum	1	2	3
Circle 1 if you find this behaviour acceptable and it wouldn't concern you at all, or hardly bother you.			
Circle 2 if this behaviour would concern you to some extent or bother you quite a lot.			
Circle 3 if this behaviour would bother you very much/give you real cause for concern.			

Behaviour	Rating		
Calling out questions/answers/comments when supposed to raise hands.	1	2	3
Looking around/looking out of window when you're talking.	1	2	3
Swinging or rocking in seat.	1	2	3
Talking out of turn (non-work-related chat).	1	2	3
Asking to leave the room frequently.	1	2	3
Humming or singing while working.	1	2	3
Chewing pencil, ruler, or hair.	1	2	3
Display of temper e.g. throwing a book on the floor, kicking desk, overturning a chair.	1	2	3
Laughing/smirking when getting a row.	1	2	3
Laughing/smirking when another child is being reprimanded.	1	2	3
Pushing/pulling/poking/nipping another child in class or line.	1	2	3
Frequently breaking and sharpening pencils.	1	2	3

'Losing' or forgetting textbooks, jotters, homework.	1	2	3
Looking blank (i.e. pretending not to understand instructions).	1	2	3
Saying 'No' to you or another adult.	1	2	3
Fighting/kicking.	1	2	3
Spitting.	1	2	3
Making faces to amuse class.	1	2	3
Swearing.	1	2	3
Smoking.	1	2	3
Making rude noises/signs.	1	2	3
Quiet/withdrawn/not joining in class activities.	1	2	3
Truanting.	1	2	3
Defacing jotters/textbooks.	1	2	3
Tapping on desk or other distracting noises.	1	2	3
Laying head on desk during lessons.	1	2	3
Saying 'that's easy' or mocking a less-able pupil.	1	2	3
Wandering aimlessly round class.	1	2	3
Calling names/teasing classmates.	1	2	3
Handing in messy/careless work.	1	2	3
Cheating or copying from neighbours.	1	2	3
Stealing.	1	2	3
Threatening other children with physical violence.	1	2	3
Constantly yawning and looking bored.	1	2	3
Asking the teacher personal questions.	1	2	3
Constantly coming in late to class.	1	2	3
Telling tales e.g. John swore in the playground. Jean's talking and not doing her work.	1	2	3
Bullying.	1	2	3
Leaving class without permission.	1	2	3

Normally when staff in a school undertake this task they find that there are certain behaviours on which there is general agreement. For example, threatening other children with physical violence is usually rated as a 3. However, there are many behaviours on the list that promote debate and it is these behaviours which evoke considerable variation in views. Most effective teachers find the task provides food for thought and a context for professional reflection. In particular the following points usually emerge. Two words which are often applied by effective teachers are 'it depends'. They want consistency but they do not want a policy that is a controlling device and does not encourage professional flexibility. They see the need to adhere to the policy as a basis for consistent action but they do not want to be reduced to robots with little or no opportunity to think for themselves. They want to be able to interpret policy as professionals and this involves some key ideas:

1 Behaviour is a relationship issue and to understand behaviour a professional must consider his behavioour as well as that of the young person.
2 Behaviour is affected by the situation in which it occurs. The context must always be taken into account.
3 It is too easy to be influenced by value judgements which can colour one's response to challenging behaviour.
4 Behaviour is complex and there is seldom one hard and fast answer. There are no quick fixes or easy solutions.

The following scenarios should hopefully help to illustrate my point.

Scenario 1 – Outdoor clothing

It has been agreed with all staff in secondary school X that young people should remove all outdoor clothing when they come into class. Mr Brown tells his third-year class to do so and reminds them that it is a school rule. The majority comply except Charlie who has just returned from a period of exclusion relating to his disruptive behaviour. This boy is not causing any disruption other than the fact he has not complied with Mr Brown's request. No other pupil has commented and so Mr Brown decides that at present he will ignore Charlie and try to get on with the lesson. He intends to speak with Charlie after the rest of the class have gone and make it clear that this behaviour is not acceptable. Mr Smith, a member of the senior management team, comes into the class to speak with Mr Brown. He sees Charlie and immediately tells him to stand up and take his outdoor jacket off. Charlie does so reluctantly murmuring under his breath. Mr Smith then quietly reminds Mr Brown about the school rule and the need for all teachers to be singing from the same hymn sheet. Mr Brown says that he was aware of and agreed with the school policy and tries to explain that he had made a professional decision given the circumstances and he did intend to deal with the matter at an appropriate time but Mr Smith simply repeated that it was school policy and left the room. Charlie and some of his classmates were obviously annoyed by what had happened and before long Mr Brown was trying to cope with some very challenging behaviour.

Reflection

- Was Mr Brown right in the way he handled this situation?
- What is your view in relation to Mr Smith's actions?
- What should Mr Brown do now?

Scenario 2 – Eating in class

In primary school X the staff have agreed that eating in class is not acceptable and this has been incorporated into the school policy. Mrs Sweeney has a Primary 4 class who are usually fairly well behaved. She is working one to one with a boy who has some learning difficulties and as she scans her classroom she sees Rachael, who is in another group, putting a sweet into her mouth.

Rachael's behaviour can be disruptive but at this point she is on task. Mrs Sweeney stops working with the pupil and tells Rachael to empty the sweet into the bin reminding her that she is breaking a school rule. Rachael swallows the sweet and says she did not have anything in her mouth. Mrs Sweeney goes over to Rachael and says she is telling a lie and that's another school rule she is breaking. Everyone in the class focuses on Rachael and Mrs Sweeny and soon a full-blown confrontation is in progress which ends with Rachael running out of the class saying she is being picked on. The class become restless and most are now off task.

Reflection

- Mrs Sweeney was keen to ensure that she followed school policy. What do you think of the strategy she used?
- How could Mrs Sweeney have followed the school policy but handled things more effectively?

These scenarios emphasise the importance of creating consistent approaches which are in line with school policy. At the same time, however, they highlight the weaknesses inherent in policies which dictate exactly how teachers should respond. Unfortunately there are still teachers who want this rigid approach and who define consistency as everyone doing the same thing all of the time. Such blinkered approaches are likely to fail because they do not incorporate an element of choice which enhances the teacher's professional role.

Theme 2 – behaviour support strategies

As mentioned previously in this chapter there are several excellent books currently on the market which outline a range of strategies which can be utilised by teachers who wish to be more effective at promoting positive behaviour. There are some key strategies which are promoted in most of these publications and in this task I have presented 30 of the most common strategies advocated.

CPD Task 2 – Bahaviour Management

Each member of staff should complete the task as an individual as follows:

- Circle 1 if this is a strategy you seldom or never use.
- Circle 2 if this is a strategy you often use.
- Circle 3 if this is a strategy you use all of the time.

Individuals should be able to provide evidence to back up their view. What would an observer in class see to show that the strategy was being used?

Staff should then share their responses and discuss their views with colleagues, the aim being to learn from each other in a supportive atmosphere which celebrates and shares good practice across the school.

Strategy	Rating		
Avoid the audience effect. Try to deal with incidents on a one-to-one basis if possible.	1	2	3
Reject the challenging behaviour not the young person.	1	2	3
Use praise and encouragement and remember all young people have strengths.	1	2	3
Treat everyone fairly, equally and maintain their dignity.	1	2	3
Avoid making threats/promises you cannot follow through.	1	2	3
Never shout or lose your temper.	1	2	3
Follow up on issues that matter. Don't get bogged down in trivial behaviours.	1	2	3
Model the behaviour you expect from young people.	1	2	3
Use humour whenever possible and if appropriate.	1	2	3
Keep corrective action as unobtrusive as possible.	1	2	3

Convey anger/frustration assertively not aggressively.	1	2	3
Always position yourself where you are aware of all activity in the classroom (scanning).	1	2	3
Use the language of choice. Ensure the young person knows he/she has choices.	1	2	3
Always try to give advice as to the behaviour expected before issuing warnings.	1	2	3
Allow time for the young person to comply with your request.	1	2	3
Listen genuinely to the young person and always try to protect their self-esteem.	1	2	3
Be firm, fair and consistent at all times. This may mean treating young people equally but differently.	1	2	3
Avoid the blame culture in relation to young people, their home and their community.	1	2	3
See behaviour as a relationship issue and repair damaged relationships as soon as possible.	1	2	3
Reflect carefully on the curriculum and be aware that it can exacerbate and alleviate disruptive behaviour.	1	2	3
Keep in mind that young people whose behaviour can be challenging may have additional support needs.	1	2	3
Always keep the focus on the primary behaviours. Do not go off at a tangent onto secondary behaviours.	1	2	3
Calm yourself before trying to calm others.	1	2	3
Eye contact is crucial. Always try to maintain it when dealing with young people.	1	2	3
Be alert and learn from your mistakes. Reflect honestly on what went wrong and what was successful. Build on strengths and overcome weaknesses.	1	2	3

Always use the young person's first name and find ways to show you are genuinely interested in them as individuals.	1	2	3
Develop your awareness of situations which may escalate into confrontation. Be proactive not reactive.	1	2	3
Appreciate the impact of the hidden curriculum.	1	2	3
Try to understand the lives the young people live and whenever possible show empathy and understanding.	1	2	3
Use gesture, body language and non-verbal cues appropriately.	1	2	3

SUMMARY

The teacher is the key individual in any classroom. The skilful teacher manages behaviour and is able to adopt strategies to suit the context in which they occur. All teachers are not equally effective in making behaviour management strategies work and those who are most able to do so display a range of characteristics. These characteristics are outlined in this chapter and the reader can audit his/her own teaching style against them.

It is very important to remember that teachers also need to feel supported, valued and have their talents recognised and those who lead the school play an important role in creating the conditions whereby this happens.

In order to fulfil this supportive motivating function senior managers must be aware of and display in practice their understanding of the distinction between management and leadership. Effective leaders demonstrate and model on a daily basis what they expect of their teachers. If they want inspirational teachers they must themselves be inspirational leaders. They must have a vision and be able to communicate it to those they lead.

There are, of course, strategies which teachers can use to promote positive behaviour. However, these will work only in the hands of teachers who are able to reflect upon their own behaviour and its effect on young people. This involves looking at their predominant management style and developing the skill of adapting this style to the prevailing circumstances.

Teachers need to be consistent in their approach and the behavioural checklist included in this chapter should help them think about this. It should also help teachers appreciate the range of behaviour management strategies they currently use and suggest a few they might develop.

POINTS FOR REFLECTION

1. Why are some teachers more successful than others at promoting positive behaviour?

2. What is the difference between management and leadership within the school context?

3. What are the main features of an effective whole school policy on behaviour/indiscipline?

8 Behaviour – the parental perspective

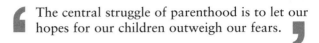

> The central struggle of parenthood is to let our hopes for our children outweigh our fears.

(Ellen Goodman)

Partnership and collaboration

In 2006 HMIE published *How good is our school? The Journey to Excellence.* This document indicates that there is no single formula for excellence in schools and that excellence is seen as a journey rather than something fixed and predetermined.

Ten dimensions are identified as the benchmarks for excellence and schools are expected to use these when they undertake their audit of current practice. These dimensions represent the features of excellence schools should strive to attain.

Some of these dimensions are underpinned by concepts such as partnership and collaboration, and there is a strong focus upon working co-operatively with young people, colleagues, parents and other professionals. Dimension six focuses upon developing parents' support for their children's learning, and in relation to disaffected young people and their parents, staff in schools are expected to establish a culture of inclusion, acceptance and positive discipline. The emphasis is placed upon reaching out to these young people and their parents to ensure they experience acceptance and success within a culture of inclusion.

In 2000 and 2003 Hamill and Boyd carried out two one-year research studies in two Scottish education authorities. The findings of these studies were presented in detailed reports to these authorities and were published by the University of Strathclyde.

In the final three chapters of this book I intend to draw upon the research findings to explore:

- the parent's perceptions in relation to the concept of disruptive behaviour and to raise the issues which are important to them (Chapter 8)
- the views of pupils who display disruptive behaviour and their peers who are not disruptive but are often on the receiving end of disruption (Chapter 9)
- the issues which need to be addressed if a holistic inter-agency approach is to become a reality (Chapter 10).

I will set the context for all three chapters at this point by describing the research.

The research

The research brief was the same for both research studies and involved a systemic approach which evaluated the nature and range of provision in mainstream schools for young people who experienced social, emotional and behavioral difficulties. An important dimension of these studies was to shed some light upon the effectiveness of in-school support systems for young people whose behaviour could be disruptive and who were often excluded. A range of methodologies was employed by the researchers and the qualitative process within schools was given priority. An in-depth study of these processes required methods that reflected their complexity. The researchers made every effort to include all significant individuals, specifically young people, parents and other professionals, and a range of research tools was employed to ensure these key players had ample opportunity to have their voices heard. Use was made of observation schedules, questionnaires, semi-structured interviews and support analysis grids. An ethnographic case study approach was used to explore how support strategies in schools had evolved, and emphasis was placed upon how pupils, their families, school and community interact. The overall study was set within an action research context which provided scope for collaboration between the researchers and those who live with, work with, and support young people whose behaviour can be complex and challenging.

Three crucial dimensions – social justice, equal opportunities and human rights – were central to the whole research process. A cycle of feedback permeated the studies creating strong links between the researchers and the school community. The intention was to empower those who supported these young people through a process of critical enquiry, helping to influence the shape of the research outcomes and hopefully provide new knowledge which could be used to transform aspects of the current systems in place. A descriptive narrative approach as outlined by Strauss and Corbin (1990) was used to analyse the qualitative data gathered. This ensured that all views were represented and these were blended into a recognisable reality, resulting in the identification of a series of recurring themes expressed and shared by a range of individuals. This involved the interpretation of a rich stream of data in a way which ensured all significant voices were heard, and which identified, on the basis of the research evidence, a number of related themes.

Twenty secondary schools were involved in the research. Questionnaires were completed by 1200 teachers, and the senior management team and behaviour support staff in all schools were interviewed. Fifty parents whose children had been excluded from school because of their challenging behaviour were interviewed. In addition, the researchers attended a meeting of the school board in each school and the parents' representatives on these boards were interviewed. As far as the pupils were concerned, 75 young people who displayed disruptive behaviour and had been excluded at some time were interviewed. To provide a more balanced picture the researchers talked with the pupils on the pupil councils and pupils who were being educated in classes which included disruptive pupils. Using an observation schedule, a sample of 25 of the excluded pupils were observed in school over the course of one full day.

In relation to both parents and pupils specific use was made of the semi-structured interviews which focused upon their perceptions in relation to areas such as teaching and learning, curriculum, exclusion, support systems and behaviour. This interview methodology was underpinned by the work of Rogers (1980), quoted in McIntyre and Cooper (1996). He suggests a range of techniques which can facilitate the interview process. These include empathy, unconditional positive regard, congruence, and repeat probing. McIntyre and Cooper take this approach a bit further when they set out a series of steps to be taken which they suggest are particularly useful when interviewing young people. These include clearly defining and enacting relationships, negotiating access and selecting relevant techniques. The researchers adhered closely to this partnership model in an attempt to ensure the interviewees saw themselves as central to the process of enquiry. All interviews were taped and the direct quotations in these chapters are taken from the interview transcripts.

More detailed information relating to these research studies can be found in the reports provided for the education authorities. If the reader would like to access these reports he/she should contact the author.

Parents and carers as partners

As far back as 1967 the *Plowden Report* (DES, 1967) recognised the impact of positive parental attitudes on educational performance and highlighted the importance of home–school partnership as a key feature of effective schools. Research evidence has continued to emphasise consistently the importance of working with parents and carers as partners (Wolfendale, 1992; Mittler and Mittler, 1994; Dowling, 2005). Armstrong (1995, p. 18) summed up the essence of this partnership when he said it involves 'mutual respect, complementary expertise and a willingness to learn from each other'. This, of course, is what can be described as the model which should underpin good practice, but this does not mean that it is evident in all schools. In some schools, parents recognise this model in action; in others it remains more at the level of rhetoric as opposed to reality.

Most schools now strive to be inclusive, and effective senior managers realise that they are first and foremost leaders who have a vision for their schools and are able to inspire their colleagues to internalise and work towards achieving this vision. An inclusive school is one in which parents also share the vision and where they are actively encouraged to express their views openly in a positive supportive atmosphere. The professionals who work in these schools realise that the building of home–school partnerships depends upon mutual commitment to a set of shared priorities and ensuring that parents have a locus within the decision-making process which affects their lives and their children's lives.

Many schools have already achieved this quality of partnership. *The Journey to Excellence* report (HMIE, 2006) gives some key features of excellent schools which work with parents to improve learning. In these schools 'what parents think is important for the school and for their own children and has a significant influence on the schools' vision. They help to formulate the school's priorities for improvement' (p. 81). Many other schools are working hard to demonstrate that they are worthy of this accolade. In these schools, the quality of leadership is a key factor along with highly committed teachers who value all parents and who strive to encourage them to play their part in the educational process. In these schools, efforts are made to ensure there is no culture of blame and there is a realisation that most parents want the best for their children and that some parents face particular barriers which can be difficult to overcome.

Unfortunately there are also still schools which have not made sufficient progress in this area and who continue to take a more minimalist approach to parental involvement. In 1999, the Scottish Council Foundation report, which considered the relationships between children, their families and the learning process, described parental participation in these less effective schools as involving no more than occasional meetings with the teacher, possibly joining the school board or the PTA plus occasional volunteer help with back-up tasks and school outings. I do not wish to imply that this minimalist approach is negative. All schools will continue to retain the positive aspects of this traditional model but as we move further into this new millennium, schools are expected to build upon this practice in a way which adds value and attains the targets now set in *The Journey to Excellence.*

In the case of some parents whose children are likely to be troublesome and disruptive in school, involving them can sometimes pose problems. It is all too easy for situations to occur which are characterised by mistrust and antagonism as opposed to collaboration and partnership. Parents can feel that they are being held totally responsible for the source of their child's behavioral difficulties and as a result they feel a bit intimidated and reluctant to come into school. Teachers, too, can feel unappreciated in situations where they perceive themselves to be isolated and unsupported. Underlying all of this is the fact that both parents and teachers can internalise a whole range of experiences, beliefs and feelings and these can pose barriers to partnership.

Hamill and Boyd were particularly keen to hear the views of as wide a range of parents as possible. This included parents whose children had been excluded from school as a result of their challenging behaviour and also parents of children who did not present challenging behaviour. Many parents in the former group could themselves be described as disaffected. Like their children, they expressed the view that in some schools they were seen as peripheral and in their opinion no real attempt was made by these schools to find out what they thought or to involve them actively in the decisions taken in relation to their children. However, in other schools they felt that they were involved and their views were treated with respect. The parents in the latter group were more involved in the work of the school and they were aware of and concerned about the negative impact of disruptive children on the school community as a whole. The views expressed by these parents throw light upon those aspects of the behavioral support systems which are working well in schools and on which aspects might be further developed. Any school striving for excellence should find this parental feedback illuminating and informative.

Parental perspectives

The researchers were concerned initially about the number of parents of the more disaffected pupils who might volunteer to be interviewed. They wrote to all parents whose children had been excluded due to behavioral difficulties and as a result, over the two studies, 50 of these parents were interviewed and their views added a vital dimension to the studies. In addition, the researchers met with the representatives on the school boards and this included an additional 55 parents. It was felt that these parents had children at the school who were not misbehaving but were being affected by the indiscipline caused by some of their peers and therefore their views were important. While Scottish school boards are not, strictly speaking, parental bodies since they have among their membership teachers and other co-optees, nevertheless the parents who stand for election are often highly motivated and willing to express their views which affect their school and their children.

Parents on school boards

These parents expressed their views in relation to a number of relevant issues.

Inclusive education

Parents were in general supportive of inclusive education in principle and felt it was a sound educational philosophy. However, there were also reservations expressed by several parents who, while agreeing with the principle underpinning exclusion, raised some issues which they felt had to be faced and resolved in the best interests of all young people. There was a feeling that the rights of those who displayed challenging behaviour often appeared to take precedence over those of their peers who were not disruptive. Thus parents qualified their support for including these more challenging pupils by saying that they would have reservations if, as a result of inclusion, their own child's education was adversely affected. The general view was that as far as possible young people who misbehave should be in the mainstream school, but that they might be best placed in an in-school behavioral unit and not necessarily in classrooms with those who did not cause disruption. Emphasis was placed on meeting the needs of the majority of young people. There were also concerns in relation to the resourcing of inclusion and there was a fairly widespread view held that inclusion was not adequately resourced. One parent summed this up as follows:

> I am a bit worried that resources do not appear to be equally shared. Some of these difficult kids seem to be getting more than their fair share and this surely has some impact on others who also require help.

In fact many parents were quite cynical and felt that inclusion was not based on the needs of young people but it was motivated by a desire to save money.

Seriously disaffected young people

The majority of parents made distinctions in relation to the levels of disruptive behaviour displayed by young people. Understandably, they were unclear about what exactly was meant by the term 'social, emotional and behavioral difficulties' but they were clear that in most schools there was a small but significant minority of pupils whose behaviour was more complex and more challenging and who in their view constantly disrupted the teaching and learning process. Many parents reported that they were aware of these situations because their own children often informed them of particularly challenging individuals who were continually disruptive. The parents were unanimous in what they thought should happen to these pupils. They considered that their needs were too complex and these young people should be educated in some form of external provision more suited to them.

Attainment

As one would expect from this group, they wanted their children to achieve their full potential and there was a strong emphasis placed upon attainment. This theme was raised on innumerable occasions and most parents had a view that the inclusion of the most seriously disruptive pupils had a direct negative effect on their peers. The following quote from a parent gets to what many parents perceive to be the heart of the matter.

> My son only gets one chance at education and I want him to get good exam results. This is the only way in the long run he is going to succeed.

The majority of these parents were well aware that attainment also covered areas such as personal and social development, social competence and inter-personal skills but the view expressed by the majority was that academic attainment was the priority.

> I know education is more than just getting good Standard Grades but in the real world that is still what counts.

The role of the teacher

All parents were very supportive of the work being done by most teachers. They fully appreciated how complex and diverse the teacher's role could be and they understood how much more difficult the job could be when trying to balance the needs of all pupils in a class which included one or two disruptive individuals. There was a realisation that time was precious and a belief that a considerable amount of teacher time went to dealing with the most disruptive pupils. Again, this was deemed to be stressful for the teacher and unfair on the other pupils. Some parents were keen to know how much training/staff development teachers received in order to help them work with and support young people whose behaviour was challenging. The parents felt that teachers also required support and that they had a right to expect that additional support and appropriate training be made available to them. However, the parents were concerned about a sizeable minority of teachers they believed to be ineffective and they thought that this group of teachers was actually adding to the problem of disruptive behavior in schools. The following two quotes should help illustrate this point.

> One teacher who shall remain nameless treats some pupils as second-class citizens and I have heard other parents say that they feel she talks down to them.

> I have heard my son say that in some classes teachers provoke the difficult kids. Maybe they just want rid of them and that can't be right.

Involving parents

The parents on the school boards recognised the importance of becoming involved in their child's education. This was the motivating force which led them to join the school board. They accepted the fact that there are still many parents who are reluctant to come into school, and although schools know the importance of getting these parents on board, it is a struggle to do so. The parents on the school boards thought that the following issues need to be considered:

- There are not enough opportunities available for parents to get to know teachers properly. The only opportunity is at the parents' night and that is not really enough time to build up any meaningful partnership.
- Some parents do not have good memories of their own school days and when they do come in to school the emphasis is on their child's problem and the parents' inadequacies.
- Not all teachers are equally skilled at making parents feel valued. Those who are good at this communicate in a way which conveys a realistic picture of the child but at the same time respects the child and the parent. These teachers need to share their skills with less effective colleagues.
- Some parents feel very anxious about the complexity of the work their children do at school. They feel unsure and a bit inadequate at times. They do not want to be made to feel stupid and teachers need to understand this and help parents feel more secure.
- Developing sound teacher–parent links is not easy especially when some parents resist the efforts made by schools to involve them. However, the school can never give up on these parents and they must always be able to show that they continue to make an effort to reach out to them. Schools should never give up on parents even if they appear to be disinterested and disaffected.

It would be fair to argue that the parents who put themselves forward for election to school boards do not necessarily represent the views of all the parents of pupils at the school. It is not my intention to make such a sweeping claim but the views these parents express provide an additional perspective which is both valid and illuminating.

Parents of children whose behaviour is disruptive

I will now turn the spotlight onto the parents of disruptive pupils, whose views are of particular relevance in relation to how schools provide for young people whose behaviour is challenging. These parents are *au fait* with the behaviour support systems set up to cater for the needs of their children and it is therefore very important that they have their say in relation to the effectiveness of these systems and that schools listen to them.

Exclusion

These parents have direct experience of the effects of exclusion both on their children and on their own lives. The vast majority were realistic about the nature and range of disruptive behaviour displayed by their children and were more than prepared to agree that they had to accept some responsibility for their child's behaviour. These parents knew only too well that on occasions the behaviour exhibited left the school with little or no alternative but to exclude the pupil. When the behaviour of their child had health and safety implications, parents were particularly supportive of the actions of the school.

> I accept he must be excluded for fighting. The last time he was excluded it was because he was swinging a chisel around in class. This was downright dangerous and I could see why he was excluded.

The culture of blame

Several parents made the point that, in their opinion, some members of the senior management team and a significant number of teachers tended to put the blame for their child's behaviour squarely upon the parent's shoulders. Most of the parents could see why this was the case but felt that, even on the occasions they were genuinely trying to do their best, the blame was laid firmly and exclusively at their door. These professionals made it abundantly clear to the parents that it was the parent who had responsibility for the problem child and it was up to him/her to sort the child out. These professionals were seen as unapproachable. They conveyed a sense of being blinkered in that they held the entrenched view that the child was trouble, and that the source of his/her undisciplined behaviour was the home and his/her ineffective parents. While it must be recognised that there are elements of truth underpinning this viewpoint, it represents only part of a wider picture and presents in itself a barrier to partnership working.

Parents tended not to try and excuse the behaviour of their child but they thought that some professionals who promoted this culture of blame were reluctant to try and understand the parent's position. To them there appeared to be reluctance on the part of these professionals to appreciate that the source of the behavioral difficulties could also reside within the school and not always the home. One parent explained her situation as follows:

> Some teachers are just not prepared to understand my problems. I am a single parent bringing up four children on my own and it is not easy. I try my best and it's not always my fault but I know that I don't cope sometimes. It's hard at times and when the kids start carrying on it can be chaos in my house.

This negative picture was counterbalanced by a contrasting, more positive view, again strongly held by some parents. There were two groups of teachers they came into contact with fairly often. These were the behaviour support teachers and the guidance teachers, and they were identified as people who were more prepared to see the bigger picture and who did not automatically assume that the parent was always at fault.

> They seem to be more understanding. They don't write me off as a failure. I know I am not the best mum but I am not the worst either.

The in-school pupil behaviour support base

All schools had in place a pupil support base which had been set up as an alternative to exclusion. The behaviour support staff who worked in these bases supported pupils who had been excluded or were in danger of being excluded. The parents of these pupils had experience of how the base operated. They understood its purpose and knew the staff well who worked there. All of these parents expressed the view that the pupil support base had, on occasions, been a lifeline for them and their child. In particular they felt that the base:

- reduced the likelihood of exclusion
- provided a vital point of contact and support for parents and young people where they could discuss problems with staff who were sympathetic and understanding
- enabled the young person to focus upon the learning task in a one-to-one or group situation
- provided a therapeutic context where young people could address their social and emotional difficulties.

Several parents concurred with the sentiments expressed by one of them:

> The base has brought him out and helped his confidence. It made him see he was not the only one with problems. He could talk openly to Mr X. The base has supported me and helped me at difficult times.

Barriers to learning

A high percentage of parents, when asked to talk about their child's behavioral difficulties, focused immediately upon what they saw as barriers to their learning as opposed to their disruptive behaviour. For many parents, low levels of literacy and numeracy were key factors, and when young people were faced with tasks which exposed their lack of skill in these areas they reacted by behaving badly in order to disguise the fact that they were experiencing difficulties. They had to save face at all costs and they did so by conveying a sense of apathy which belittled the impossible tasks expected of them. This helped to conceal their deep-rooted sense of anxiety and vulnerability.

> When he gets work he can't do he causes trouble. He can't cope and he can't lose face in front of his pals.

These parents were not necessarily blaming the school and they realised that the reasons for their child's misbehaviour were complex. Their aim was to point out that there were also school-based issues which were largely outwith their control. The parents were very appreciative of the support many teachers provided, but they wanted to make the point that there were sometimes more reasons as to why a child might misbehave in school. Focusing too rigidly on the perceived inherent deficiencies residing within the child can obstruct one's view of the real issues.

> I know X is bad a lot of the time but it's not always his fault. If he is put under pressure to do things he can't he will eventually explode. I don't like this but I understand how he feels sometimes.

The teacher is the key

The parents were generally complimentary in relation to the quality of support provided by most teachers. Understandably, they had most contact with behaviour support teachers, support for learning teachers and guidance teachers and in general they were keen to praise specifically the input of these specialist staff. With regard to classroom teachers, they had established very clear perceptions in relation to those seen to be child-centred as opposed to subject-centred. These pupil-orientated teachers were deemed not only to respect pupils, but they were also deemed to value parents.

> Mr X never talks down to me. He listens to what I have to say and he understands my views. He doesn't always agree with me but at least I feel he respects me and wants to do the best for my boy.

The parents were more than prepared to support this kind of teacher, and they were aware that teaching was a demanding job and that some young people who were disruptive put considerable additional demands upon teachers. Although there was support for those who the parents perceived to be effective teachers, a significant minority of teachers were identified as individuals who were themselves disaffected and this adversely affected their pupils.

> As well as hearing about badly behaved pupils there are also some teachers who in my opinion are badly behaved and don't value or respect pupils.

Some parents also made the point that they felt that it was all too easy in some schools for a young person to be firmly labelled as disruptive. When this happened, they felt that it was virtually impossible for the young person to dispel this negative reputation. Once in the cycle of disruption, it was difficult for the young person to escape. Some teachers were prepared to try and offer another chance to the young person, but for some, the young person was responsible for the reputation they had acquired and they treated them accordingly. Sometimes this reputation had been earned in primary school and came with the child at the transition stage.

Attention deficit/hyperactivity disorder (AD/HD)

A number of parents mentioned that their child had been diagnosed with AD/HD and there were some young people who had been prescribed the drug Ritalin. These parents were at pains to emphasise that these young people found it difficult to control their behaviour due to this condition.

> I have three children but he is the only one who gets excluded and causes problems.

These parents expressed the view that most teachers did not really understand what it meant to have AD/HD and they described occasions when they felt some teachers were dismissive of the condition and conveyed the opinion that AD/HD was just used as a smokescreen for parents and the pupil to avoid facing the real problem.

> When I mention AD/HD to some teachers I get the feeling that they just see it as a cover up and ignore it because in fact he is just a bad boy.

Drugs and alcohol

This was something about which all parents expressed real concern. It was clear that drug and alcohol abuse was an area which worried parents and was a constant source of anxiety. Parents agreed unanimously that this was one of the biggest worries they faced.

> I hear the kids where I live talk about hash as if it's just another cigarette. It's not and it's not hard to see where it leads. Alcohol is seen as an every day thing. Every time I go to the shops I see kids drinking wine.

Fostering

Several of the parents interviewed had experience of fostering and provided evidence that the young person had been adversely affected by inappropriate parenting and lack of love in the early years.

> When I go to the school I want to tell the teachers about X's life. He has never had a real home or caring parents until now. I am doing what I can but it's not enough.

These foster parents are to be highly commended for the way they care for these young people who are often troubled. This issue also brings to the fore the importance of inter-profession collaboration and the need to consider more carefully the nature and range of additional support these young people require.

There can be no doubt that the job of parenting in today's complex society is particularly difficult. Dowling (2005) emphasises the need for all agencies working with parents to respect and support the family unit. Katz (1995) highlights the diversity in family patterns within society and points out that it is not the particular pattern which impacts on the child's social and emotional development but the quality of care and support which matters most.

Working with parents, carers and families is complex and schools have a unique role to play respecting, supporting and informing parents throughout their child's school life. To do so they must listen actively to parents and, where it is appropriate and possible, show that they are taking on board what parents say.

 **SUMMARY**

For over 40 years it has been recognised that when parents work in partnership with teachers, young people's educational attainment is enhanced. Schools can no longer operate effectively if they do not make every effort to ensure their parents are on board. The report *How good is our school? The Journey to Excellence* (HMIE, 2006) gives a very high priority to linking home and school.

Some schools have already gone a long way to ensure parents have a voice in the decision-making process. However, others still have some way to go and the relationship between the home and the school is less positive than it might be.

One group of parents who can easily become isolated and alienated are those whose children display challenging behaviour. These parents often think that schools blame them for their children's misbehaviour. While it must be accepted that they have a responsibility in this matter, the 'blame culture' does not help to move things forward.

Hamill and Boyd conducted research which evaluated the nature and range of provision in mainstream for young people whose behaviour could be challenging. As part of this research they attempted to ascertain the views of parents whose children were not disruptive and parents whose children were disruptive. The aim was to give parents a voice. The range of views expressed was very enlightening and they are detailed in this chapter. Hopefully schools, and particularly those responsible for policy development, will take some of these views on board when considering how best to ensure that parental partnership is genuinely alive and well.

POINTS FOR REFLECTION

1 How effective are schools at actively canvassing the views and opinions of parents, particularly in relation to the quality of education and the running of the school?

2 Is there an additional effort made to involve parents who themselves have become disaffected and who have for whatever reason internalised negative feelings about schools and schooling?

3 Should professionals in schools bring together parents with specific needs and common interests to form support groups and forums which would be of benefit to these particular parents and their children?

9 Behaviour – the young person's voice

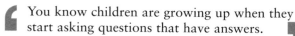

> You know children are growing up when they start asking questions that have answers.

(John L Plomb)

Overview

In this chapter, I will continue to draw upon the research evidence emanating from the two research studies undertaken by Hamill and Boyd. The researchers realised that young people in school were likely to have a certain perspective in relation to why young people misbehave and the impact this had on the learning and teaching process. In order to ensure that the picture that emerged was as comprehensive as possible, three groups of young people were interviewed:

1 Members of the school council representing all year groups.
2 Pupils who were being educated in classes alongside those in group 3.
3 Pupils who had experience of being excluded due to their disruptive behaviour.

I will in the first instance look at the views expressed by groups 1 and 2 and then go on to consider the views held by group 3.

Listening to the pupil

Over the past few years, an increasing priority has been given to children's rights, and within this context young people are now expected to be seen and heard. This emphasis on rights, which is now high on the educational agenda, was given real priority for the first time in 1990 by the United Nations Convention on Human Rights Article 12, which asserts that the child has the right to express his/her opinion in all matters affecting her/him. In 2000, the Standards in Scotland's Schools Etc. Act extended these rights in relation to school development and education authority plans which have an impact upon the young person's quality of life. This process of actively encouraging young people to have their say evolved gradually, and it is interesting to consider this evolution briefly in order to provide some background information which should help set the discussion in this chapter in context.

Historical perspective

As early as 1978, an organisation entitled 'Who Cares? Scotland' took a major step forward when they considered the provision for young people who were in the care of the local authority. It was recognised that this was a particularly vulnerable group of young people whose opinions were rarely, if ever, asked for even when major life-changing decisions were being made in relation to them. This forward-looking organisation highlighted the need to give these young people an opportunity to speak up, particularly in relation to issues which affected their lives.

1995 saw the setting up of 'Connect Youth', which was a national initiative whose aim was to promote the rights of Scotland's youth. A national network was put in place which provided a forum where young people could share their views and exchange ideas which would help shape good practice, and in 1999 the 'Scottish Youth Parliament' was established. This youth parliament played an influential role in promoting change.

The year 2000 was a watershed year when matters came to a head with the proposal from the 'Scottish Alliance for Children's Rights' for a commissioner for children in Scotland. This commissioner would be an independent voice and an advocate for children's rights.

From all this, it is clear that things have moved in the right direction. However, we still have some way to go and, despite the emphasis placed on the underpinning theory, the good practice relating to children's rights is still not a reality for some young people. Too many remain silent and are not in a position to influence the policies and practices which shape their lives. These young people are often members of families who are socially excluded and disadvantaged. The needs of these young people are in danger of becoming less important and are often overlooked.

It would not be accurate to suggest that all of the young people who are excluded from schools because of their disruptive behaviour come from socially deprived families. However, Hamill and Boyd (2000; 2003) found that when they considered the characteristics of young people who were repeatedly excluded, the majority had difficulty developing social competences, adjusting to social contexts and learning to follow normal and accepted behavioural patterns. In addition, many of these young people did come from dysfunctional families, had input from social work and psychological services and had come into contact with the police due to their behaviour in the wider community.

These young people are now recognised has having additional support needs (special educational needs) and the *Code of Practice* published in 2005 by the Scottish Executive sets out guidance for local authorities and other agencies in respect of their duties relating to the Education (Additional Support for Learning) (Scotland) Act 2004. Consultation with young people is a theme which permeates the *Code of Practice* and is specifically addressed in Chapter 6 of the *Code* where the following important points are emphasised:

- All children and young people should have the opportunity to make their views known about decisions which affect them. They should have the opportunity to express these opinions and have these opinions taken seriously.
- Some children and young people with additional support needs will be able to express themselves clearly and directly. All they may need are opportunities and encouragement to do so. Other children and young people may need support with communication or confidence to express their views. Very few will be unable to express a view at all.
- In order to express views, children and young people need to have experience of being asked for their views, being listened to, making some choices and having some influence over what they do. Schools and early settings should create a climate

where seeking children's views and encouraging participation in decision-making are part of everyday activities

(SE, 2005, p. 81–2)

Hamill and Boyd (2002; 2003) found many of the young people they interviewed to be articulate. It was particularly surprising to discover that those young people who were considered to be troubled and disaffected were keen to express their views when given the opportunity. All of the young people had issues they wanted to raise and share with others and there were clear messages for all of the professionals who worked with young people.

Young people in groups I and 2 – emerging issues

In this section I will consider the views expressed by the young people on the school councils and those who were not disruptive but were in class with some young people whose behaviour was challenging.

Inclusion

The majority of young people in these groups readily accepted that including individuals with additional support needs was in principle a commendable approach. They understood that some of their peers experienced difficulties which could pose barriers in relation to their learning. However, these young people also made it clear that when they expressed support for inclusion they mainly had in mind particular groups of their peers. They focused upon young people with learning difficulties and difficulties linked to sensory/physical difficulties. They made a distinction between these young people and those whose behaviour was challenging. The disruptive behaviour of the latter group was seen to have a negative impact not only on their own learning, but also the learning of others in the class. The more disruptive pupils were seen to demand attention and took up much more than their fair share of teacher time.

> A few people misbehave in all my classes. It's the same people over and over again. They want all the attention and take up too much of the teacher's time.

A consistent theme raised by many in these groups was the effect indiscipline had on the quality of their learning experiences. Most individuals understood that some of their more disruptive peers might have other social and emotional problems in their life outwith school. They were sympathetic but a strong view emerged that including some young people whose behaviour constantly caused disruption was not always in the best interests of their peers.

Putting up with it

The word 'bad' was often used when these young people spoke about their peers who had been excluded due to their challenging behaviour.

> There are some bad people in one of my classes and they just want to cause trouble.

When this label was further explored to clarify what was meant by 'bad' pupils, the following points were made. 'Bad' pupils:

- do not follow school rules
- shout out, swear and disrespect teachers
- destroy things, waste time and want attention all the time
- try to keep others off their work
- truant, fight and sometimes bully others.

When asked if they thought they could do anything about this, the young people painted a fairly bleak but realistic picture. They knew that often, time was of the essence and some individuals consistently wasted it. The non-disruptive pupils in these classes conveyed a sense of resignation and felt powerless to rectify the situation. They did not see that they had any choice other than to accept the situation as inevitable.

> You just have to ignore it and turn yourself off to what is going on around you. Trying to focus on your work is not easy. This is just the way it is in some classes and you just have to put up with it.

These young people agreed that they had the right to a good education but it seemed to them that there were definite occasions when it seemed that the rights of their badly behaved peers were given higher priority. However, it would appear that not all pupils are on the receiving end of disruptive behaviour; some have to tolerate much more than others, depending on the methods of organisation the school uses.

Setting and streaming

Many schools use setting and streaming as a strategy aimed at providing circumstances conducive to developing potential and raising attainment. While it may be argued that the theory underpinning these approaches may benefit many pupils, for some it may simply compound their problems. Some young people could see clearly that setting and/or streaming had a positive effect on them.

> As you move up the school you can move into better sections where everyone is trying their best so you don't have much disruption and this helps you learn.

Several of the pupils who were members of school councils made the case that if a pupil was deemed to be academic she/he benefited more from setting and streaming and it was less likely that their education would be disrupted.

It would be a sweeping generalisation to suggest that all behaviourally challenged pupils find their way into the so-called bottom sets, but it is fair to conclude that many of these young people also find learning difficult and so are more likely to be found in these sets. When the researcher observed some of these disruptive pupils in class, they found that the pupil composition of the bottom set remained fairy constant and the same pupils appeared consistently in the lower set regardless of the subject discipline. It was, in fact, the more vulnerable young people in these sets who did not misbehave who were most adversely affected.

> I am not very good at my work and I am in the Foundation group.
> That's the bottom group. I want to try and learn so that I can get
> a good job but in most of my classes you don't learn much
> because of the people who carry on all the time.

It would appear that as a result of the setting/streaming process
some young people find themselves in the lowest streams and are
placed there because, in theory, it will benefit them educationally.
The reality may be very different and many of these vulnerable
young people perceive themselves to be in ghetto classes where
they face even further barriers to their learning.

A supportive curriculum

Several young people proved to be particularly insightful in
relation to potential sources of behavioural difficulties, and
sometimes they thought that the curriculum on offer exacerbated
behavioural difficulties. These views echoed the research
literature (Cole *et al.*, 1998; Montgomery, 1998; Olsen and
Cooper, 2001) which point to the effect on behaviour of an
inappropriate curriculum. A number of these young people made
the connection between better learning and better behaviour.

> In one of my classes there is a boy who misbehaves all the time.
> He doesn't seem able to do the work and he keeps asking for help.
> I think one of the reasons he carries on is to hide his learning
> difficulties.

There was also a feeling that teachers varied in their efforts to
provide additional support and although the young people did
not use the word 'differentiation' they felt that in too many
classes everyone was expected to do the same level of work
which was demotivating, repetitive, and lacked interest,
innovation and creativity.

A significant contributory factor which either reduced or
promoted challenging behaviour was the way teachers
interpreted their role. Most of the young people could see that
the teacher's job was complex and stressful.

> A lot of the teachers in this school are really great. They have a
> hard job and have to put up with a lot. They have a stressful job.
> I wouldn't want their job.

Having said this, however, there was also a considerable amount of evidence from these interviews to suggest that in the opinion of these young people not all teachers are equally effective at promoting positive behaviour.

> Mr X shouts all the time. You get the feeling he just couldn't care less and wonder why he ever became a teacher. Behaviour in his class is awful and it's always the pupils' fault. Sometimes it's his fault. Maybe he should be excluded.

These young people wanted to be fair to their teachers and they acknowledged that teachers like Mr X were in the minority. Some teachers were weak, some were mediocre, some were good and some were excellent.

> Why can't all teachers be like Mrs X? She goes out of her way to help everyone. She makes learning interesting and fun. I've thought about being a teacher and if it happens I want to be like her.

Gender

The majority of young people who displayed disruptive behaviour in the sample schools were boys. The researchers therefore raised the issue of the effect of gender on behaviour and attainment, and the opinions of the boys and girls in these groups varied quite markedly. The boys felt they got a raw deal and that the girls had an easier life.

> If a boy and girl do the same thing they are treated differently. Girls get away with a lot more.
>
> (Boy)

Girls expressed a different view focusing on the boy's inability to look ahead and appreciate the long-term value of education. Many boys were considered to be immature, lacking in interpersonal skills and unable to control their behaviour.

> Boys want to show off and carry on. Girls set goals and work towards them. Boys say 'I'll have a laugh first'.
>
> (Girl)

A few girls felt that boys were definitely more predisposed to disruptive behaviour and they were a source of distraction in class. These individuals felt that they could develop their potential more fully in a single sex class.

> If for example I was giving a talk to the class, some of the boys would make fun but most of the girls would support each other.

It is sensible to sound a cautionary note at this point and one must be very careful what one reads into and takes from these comments. They have validity because they are genuine views expressed to the interviewers, but they are presented mainly for critical professional reflection and consideration.

Young people in group 3 – emerging issues

In this section I will consider the views of young people whose behaviour is disruptive and who have at some time been excluded from school.

Equality, fairness and rights

This group of young people tended to agree that in certain circumstances exclusion was an effective strategy. They openly discussed occasions when they had been excluded and they could see that their behaviour had not been acceptable and that exclusion was the only feasible response.

> I got excluded for shouting and arguing with the teacher and for fighting with X. I know that I did wrong and I can accept that I should have been excluded.

However, the young people did not always see the situation in this way. They could easily identify incidents when, in their view, they were not shown the respect they thought they deserved. The young people consistently used words like 'equality', 'fairness' and 'rights' when they were describing incidents which, in their opinion, resulted in exclusions which were biased and based on a one-sided teacher view. The young people expressed anger and felt they were victims of prejudice and discrimination. On these occasions they felt they were being unjustly treated and, even though they knew that the likely result would be exclusion, they still challenged what they perceived to be the teacher's misuse of power.

> I always argue with teachers who don't treat me fairly. I like teachers who respect you and don't just automatically blame you. Mr X treats everyone equally but Mr Y does not.

Being treated disrespectfully was clearly seen by these young people as a provocation to disruptive behaviour. This view is supported by Tattum (1982), Olsen and Cooper (2001) and Davies (2005). Conversely, when these young people were treated with genuine positive regard they responded accordingly (Cooper *et al.*, 2000). Several saw themselves as victims who were picked upon and made scapegoats. When the young people expressed this view, it was usually associated with specific teachers who they thought showed by their actions that they did not value the pupil. On occasions the less effective teachers were seen to be adding fuel to the fire.

> He blames me for everything. I don't get a chance to give my view and I am just thrown out of class. He treats me like shit.

It appeared to be all too easy to establish a reputation as being disruptive and for some it seemed difficult to shed this image. According to several pupils, when teachers internalise these negative perceptions it adversely affects their ability to interact positively with a young person and negatively colours their attitudes and expectations.

> If you get a reputation like me then you have no chance as far as some teachers are concerned. If there is trouble then the finger is always pointed at me even when it's nothing to do with me.

One measure of how inclusive a school is, is the extent to which individuals feel that they are valued equally (Thomas *et al.*, 1998). Some young people felt that the theory of equality was often paid lip service and it was actions which spoke much louder than words.

> It's not true to say that everyone is equally valued in this school. You can tell by the way some teachers treat some pupils that they see them as not worth bothering about.

Cullingford (1999) explored the causes of exclusion and many of his findings are mirrored in the words of these young people. He discusses issues such as reaction to teachers, disengagement from school, truancy, alienation and loss of self-esteem, and confirms the view of these young people that exclusion is complex and that great care must be taken to ensure all the factors have been considered before taking this last resort.

Doing the work

Several young people in this group were underachieving and a significant number appeared to have some difficulty learning. The young people made clear the link between misbehavior and learning difficulties. They tended to describe what they were expected to do in class as the 'work'.

> I hate it when I am in the group and I can't do the work. It's really embarrassing and I feel terrible. If people laugh at me I lose my temper and then I am sent to the Pupil Support Base.

Some teachers on the other hand are seen to be extremely supportive.

> Mr X knows I am dyslexic. He doesn't shout at me and he explains things and helps me get it right. He makes me feel that I can do it and I don't get put out of his class.

Again this relationship between learning difficulties is borne out in the literature (Garner, 1999; Pomeroy, 2000). Porter (2007) sums it up by saying that a relevant curriculum can be a preventative measure in relation to disruptive behaviour. Thomas and Loxley (2004) talk about making school more humane. They point out that some children may be disruptive because of a school culture which focuses on their problems, rather than on problems relating to professional bureaucracy and systems which aggravate difficult behaviour.

The pupil support base

All of the schools involved in the research had a pupil support base set up to provide in-school support for young people with social, emotional and behavioural difficulties. All of the young people in group 3 had direct involvement with the base provision and were keen to pass on to the researchers their experiences. They spoke very highly of the support they received and consistently focused on the behavioural support staff who worked in the base and the quality of their contribution. A fine line was drawn between these teachers who worked in and managed the pupil support base and some of the class teachers who were seen to lack empathy and understanding.

> Mrs X in the base is the best teacher in this school. She knows all about me and my problems. I can talk to her and tell her anything. She listens and understands. She can be strict as well as fair.

Several individuals felt that on occasions the base had been a lifeline which prevented them from being excluded. For them it did provide an alternative to exclusion and an opportunity to have some time out where they could cool down and talk with the base staff about coping strategies that might help them avoid confrontation in the future.

> I would be out of this school a lot more if I did not have the base to go to. It helps me cool down and avoid the trouble spots like Mrs X's class.

These pupils made it clear that they were not excluded from all classes and the reasons they gave for this was what they saw as the varying levels of teacher effectiveness. Some teachers were seen to use the base inappropriately. It was for them the first resort and they were seen to take this course of action almost immediately rather than try and resolve matters in the situation where the behavioural incident occurred.

> Mr X is not a good teacher. He can't handle the class. He shouts all the time and puts you out of the class for anything.

> Mrs X said she was not here to teach people like me. I had only stepped over the door and she said 'Base!'

Some of these young people also admitted that they preferred being in the base and sometimes they deliberately misbehaved in order to be sent out of class. This was because they felt more secure in the base and the ethos they experienced there was supportive.

> Sometimes I don't like the teacher or the subject is too boring. I cause trouble so that I can get sent to the base.

The behaviour support teachers were well aware that this could happen and on occasions they took the pupil in but ensured that they still undertook the tasks expected with some additional help. Whenever possible the behaviour support teacher worked co-operatively with the teacher and the pupil remained in class.

The pupil support base did appear to play a part in reducing exclusions but there were situations in which the base could not be seen as an alternative to exclusion and some behaviour was acknowledged as extreme, especially where it endangered the young person or others.

> I got excluded for hanging someone over the school balcony by his legs. I know this is daft and dangerous and I was excluded.

In the wider area of school effectiveness research the absence of the young person's voice has been an issue for the past twenty years. Nieto (1994, p. 396) argues that: 'one way of beginning the process of changing schools policies is to listen to the students' views about them; however research that focuses on student voices is relatively rare and scarce'. The research by Hamill and Boyd (2000; 2003) allowed the young person's voice to be heard. Young people want to have their say and it is very important to keep in mind that what they say may or may not correspond to the viewpoint and experiences of the professionals. Nonetheless, we must listen to them because their perceptions are valid and what they have to say as educational consumers provides insight into how systems operate and how they might develop in the future.

SUMMARY

Pupil councils have become a prominent feature in most schools and listening to the views of young people is now accepted as good practice. The concept of 'rights' is now emphasised and the additional support needs code of practice places a responsibility upon schools to ensure children in need have the opportunity to be actively involved in decisions which impact upon them.

Many schools have taken up this challenge and there is evidence that they take their responsibilities very seriously. These schools understand that they cannot hope to be effective unless they put the young person at the centre.

Some other schools accept the theory of pupil partnership, but it still remains at this theoretical level. In practice, little has actually changed and partnership with pupils tends to be based on rhetoric rather than reality. Hamill and Boyd wanted to ensure that the young person's voice was heard in relation to their research. Consequently, they provided opportunities for young people to express their views in relation to challenging behaviour and its impact upon their lives. The views of a wide range of young people were included – both those whose behaviour could be disruptive and those who were not disruptive but were often on the receiving end of disruption.

In this chapter these views are expressed very eloquently and, hopefully, professionals reading them will be prepared to take a step back and reflect upon the messages these young people convey.

POINTS FOR REFLECTION

1   Should young people continue to be seen and not heard? What can they tell professionals which might cause them to reflect more critically on their current practice?

2   What are the roles/functions of a pupil council? How do schools ensure that these councils are representative of the diverse school population?

3   Some young people become disaffected and marginalised in school and find it difficult to conform. They often have a different but valid view to express. What opportunities exist for them to do so?

10 Inter-professional collaboration – the extended support team

> Good inter-agency co-operation improves co-ordination, efficiency and effectiveness; reduces frustration between professionals from different disciplines and makes better use of existing resources.

(SOEID, 1998, p. 18)

Multidisciplinary working

Increasing emphasis is now placed upon inter-professional collaboration and this theme has permeated many educational reports published in recent years. In 1999, new community schools were heralded as the way forward. Those who advocated such initiatives felt schools would be able to play their part in relation to tackling social exclusion, reducing pupil disaffection and raising attainment for all. The *New Community Schools – The Prospectus* (SO, 1999) emphasised that schools alone could not combat the intractable problems relating to poverty, underachievement and indiscipline. These things could only be effectively addressed if multidisciplinary inter-agency working became the norm. Pilot community schools were set up bringing together professionals in teams and, for a while, these teams tried to develop integrated approaches aimed at destroying the cycle of underachievement and ensuring all young people maximised their full potential. It was acknowledged at the outset that achieving this level of professional integration would require fairly radical strategies. In reality these strategies never really materialised; a few interesting projects did emerge but the community school initiative did not take off as expected. However, the fundamental principles underpinning the concept of the community school are sound and continue to be given high priority on the educational agenda.

In 2001, multidisciplinary working was given prominence by the Discipline Task Group who published the *Better Behaviour – Better Learning* report (SEED, 2001). The group found that it was rare for a young person presenting challenging behaviour to do so as the result of one simple issue. One key recommendation of the report was that it is 'important that professionals with a range of different expertise are involved in assessing and supporting young people and their families' (p. 46).

The *Count Us In* report (HMIE, 2002) also focused on the importance of joined-up working involving a range of professionals. This report outlined a number of key features which are evident when good inter-agency practice exists. The emphasis was on ensuring that there was in place 'a shared clarity of purpose and good liaison between different professionals, for example social workers, community education workers, teachers and police' (p. 24).

The *Supporting Children's Learning: Code of Practice* (SE, 2005) highlights the need for integrated services and this is vital in relation to developing co-ordinated support plans and collaborative interagency partnerships. Young people with more complex wide-ranging needs will require these co-ordinated plans, and this could involve some whose additional support needs are due to the social, emotional and behavioral difficulties they experience. The needs of these young people are diverse and can influence all areas of their lives including school, home and the community. It seems logical, therefore, to conclude that many of these young people will need the support of several professionals, not as an option, but as a vital prerequisite to ensuring they are able to access, in a well co-ordinated way, the full range of services they require.

All of this relates to the discussion in Chapter 2 on systemic theory which encourages professionals to take a holistic view of behaviour. This involves looking at behaviour as it occurs in different environments and considering the interaction between these differing contexts. For such approaches to bear fruit, it is vital that all relevant professionals bring their skills together to support the young person. The rhetoric underpinning effective inter-professional partnership is easy to express; the reality is at times a very different matter. Outlining the theory behind community schools, inter-agency teamwork and multidisciplinary working does not bring to the fore the barriers which can hinder the translation of these theories into practice. As part of their research studies Hamill and Boyd (2000; 2003) interviewed a range of professionals using semi-structured interview schedules and focus group discussion. Data was collected from the following professional groups:

- education welfare officers
- community education workers
- educational psychologists
- youth strategy social workers
- family service social workers
- children's reporter and members of the children's panel
- police officers
- teachers.

Systems in place were examined from the perspective of these stakeholders and the focus was on the collaborative inter-agency dimension and in particular on the barriers which have an impact on the development of these partnerships and ultimately the quality of support young people receive.

Potential barriers

Merging professional skills

The needs of young people who experience social, emotional and behavioral difficulties can be complex and there is no one professional group within which all of the necessary skills reside. The difficulties these young people experience are evident in all areas of their lives including school, home and the community. Often they have to do their best to cope with life in a dysfunctional family and for some it appears to be hard to survive the rigours of such an existence. One young girl described her life in fairly harrowing terms:

> My brother is in prison, he's a heroin addict and my real dad died because he drank too much. I couldn't live with my mum and her boyfriend so I've got foster parents. I'd like to live my life over again.

This scenario encapsulates the need for professionals to pool their skills to benefit these young people, and sometimes they can be a bit reluctant to do so as it can be seen as a dilution of their skills. This is a restricted view and it must be challenged if we are to move beyond entrenched traditional practices. It is important to emphasise that the unique role played by specialists such as social workers, educational psychologists and community education workers can be recognised and retained while at the same time skills are merged for the good of the young person. In this way professional skills are seen to be complementary as opposed to interchangeable. The majority of the professionals who took part in the research studies (Hamill and Boyd, 2000; 2003) consistently demonstrated that they had internalised the view that all young people had a right to an appropriate education and the fundamental aim for all young people was to provide opportunities to develop their potential and raise their levels of attainment.

However, some professionals were very keen to identify aspects of their particular specialist skills. The youth strategy social workers emphasised their skills in relation to therapeutic intervention which they felt created the conditions wherein effective learning could thrive. This view was presented by one social worker thus:

> All of the therapeutic work we do is ultimately about developing potential and strategies kids can use to get the best from their education. When we work in schools our roles are to help them look for strategies they can use in class.

The community education workers also emphasised their therapeutic role and their skills in areas such as anger management and solution-focused brief therapy. They tended to work in a less formal way with young people in schools but felt that the work they did was vital to the emotional well-being of the young person and helped to equip them to cope with confrontational situations both in and outwith the classroom.

> We have to look at the underlying anger management issues and help them to develop coping strategies. Without these they will have difficulty learning anything.

The educational psychologists discussed a range of skills relating directly to their profession. They consistently mentioned their skill as counsellors working one to one with individual pupils getting them to try and confront more deep rooted issues:

> Psychologists can get to the underlying causes of disruptive behaviour and advise on how best to manage a child in class.

They were less inclined to give priority to working in class *with* teachers and saw themselves as advisors providing expert guidance *to* teachers.

Throughout these research studies the teacher's role was highlighted repeatedly and the extensive range of skills demonstrated was recognised by parents, other professionals and the young people themselves. Teachers were seen to be the group of professionals who were consistently on the front line and who had the most direct on-going experience of behaviour which was disruptive. One parent provided a comprehensive picture which showed a real understanding of life for many teachers:

> I have nothing but praise for the majority of teachers. My child has benefited from the excellent levels of support provided. Their job is not easy ... They always do their best often under difficult circumstances. My son causes problems, I know that. I would lose my patience in five minutes. I take my hat off to the teachers.

It is clear all professionals have relevant skills, and to provide effective support for troubled and troublesome young people involves multidisciplinary teamwork which enables the merging of these skills. All professionals need to accept that it is unprofessional not to engage in inter-agency joined-up working. It is only if this becomes a reality that professionals will utilise their talents collectively to benefit the young person.

The professional hierarchy

All professionals are human and it is important that their professional input is equally valued. These studies found evidence which suggests that some professionals feel their contributions are not recognised as being of equal worth and that this was mostly evident when they were working in schools.

They talked about the existence of professional hierarchies operating in schools where teachers tended to see themselves at the top and other professionals were placed lower down the hierarchy and, consequently, they perceived their input as being somewhat devalued. This was not the case, however, in all schools and a clear distinction was made between schools. A community education worker expanded on this point by saying:

> My input in schools depends very much on the school. In some I feel as if I am a valued member of the team, in others I feel a bit like a second-class citizen.

Several professionals from all groups expressed similar views and indicated that their role in some schools was peripheral and that they felt like outsiders as opposed to team members. Situations like this should be considered very seriously and action must be taken to address the inherent negative attitudes which are central to the resolution of this issue. If the situation remains unresolved it will continue to have a profound effect on in-school behaviour support systems which depend on positive professional partnerships in order for them to operate successfully.

The inclusive philosophy

Effective inclusive practice will thrive in an atmosphere where professionals agree upon and are prepared to share the philosophy which underpins that practice (Cooper *et al.*, 2000; Mittler, 2000). The concept of inclusion was a central feature of both research studies (Hamill and Boyd, 2000; 2003) and permeated all levels of enquiry. It was important, therefore, to ascertain the extent to which the professionals involved had internalised the same philosophical viewpoint. From the wide range of views expressed, it became very clear that all of the professional groups did not appear to share the same vision in relation to inclusion and evidence to support this came from a number of individuals. The first comment comes from a social worker and conveys the principle on which inclusion is based. This view, however, is contradicted to some extent by the comments which follow later.

We have always accepted the youth strategy principles which emphasised that as far as possibly all young people should stay in their homes and in their own community and school.

(Social Worker)

As far as I am concerned it is all about saving money. The kids come second, the budget first. [The emphasis is on how] much could be saved by bringing children back from residential schools.

(Educational Psychologist)

Including children is not necessarily the answer. Some schools may in fact not be doing the best for a child by making every effort to maintain him in mainstream. I sometimes suspect a political agenda rather than a child-focused one.

(Community Education Worker)

It would appear that there is some discrepancy in the way professionals perceive inclusion. There is evidently still a need for professionals to explore in more depth the concept of inclusion and reach some consensus on what it means and how it should operate – not just in principle, but in practice.

Meeting needs

Meeting the needs of young people who display challenging and disruptive behaviour involves professionals working together in a co-ordinated manner. Two aspects emerged from these research studies which signal the need to think more carefully about how professional attitudes are shaped.

Different perspectives

A concern which consistently emerged when interviewing the range of professionals was the extent to which inter-professional teamwork was a reality. There was a fairly widely held view that there was often more talk than action in relation to teamwork, and although the term 'joined-up working' is currently in vogue, it still appeared to be less evident in practice. There appeared to be issues which need to be addressed relating to the overall co-ordination of the services provided which was seen to be a bit haphazard and random as opposed to being joined up.

All professionals do not take the same view when considering the concept of need, and this view has been shaped as a result of their own professional experiences and is often deeply rooted in the different forms of initial training they have undergone. This difference of perspective can have a particular impact on how the needs of those who experience social, emotional and behavioral difficulties are identified and assessed. The professionals indicated by their responses that they each operated according to a hierarchy of need, and this hierarchy was used to prioritise which individuals were assisted first.

It is not always easy to perceive how this hierarchy works in reality because it is based upon professional perceptions which are inherent and subtle in the way they translate into practice. For the teacher, the main priority might be the need for the young person to be literate and numerate; for the social worker, the priority need might be for a stable family life; for the psychologist, the concern is to enhance a damaged self-esteem; and for the community education worker, the emphasis is on disruptive acts in the local community. All of these perspectives are valid and they show how complex the needs of some young people can be. However the constant factor for all professionals is that it is the same young person they are working with and they must find a way of meeting the range of needs holistically. It is the whole person who matters not the sum of the parts.

There was some evidence from the research studies to suggest that when professionals are unable to reconcile differing professional perspectives, the result can be inter-professional suspicion and frustration, and that this has adverse spin-offs in relation to the quality of support some vulnerable young people receive. Several professionals were very keen to make the point that the young person was too often seen as a problem to be solved by one or other particular professional group:

> The best interests of the child are not always paramount. The education department see it as a social work problem and social work see it as an education problem.
>
> (Member of a Children's Panel)

> Sometimes even at council level when different professionals meet hostile views can be expressed and a fairly cynical view taken in

relation to the different roles. There is often a feeling that one perspective is the current and dominant one and others are in some way subsidiary. This is my experience at that level.

(Social Worker)

Different contexts

It is clear that professionals, who provide support for young people whose behaviour can be disruptive, work in different contexts e.g. home, school and the community.

Each professional is usually very well aware of their context and the factors within it which pose challenges for them. It is also true that most professionals are less aware of the contexts in which others work, and this can lead to misunderstanding and misconceptions across professional groups. This is an area which is worthy of further in-depth analysis and reflection, as it can be a potential source of inter-professional conflict.

Schooling is compulsory and young people are obliged by law to attend. This does not mean that all young people are happy to attend school and in every school there are young people who, to say the least, attend reluctantly. Some do, of course, vote with their feet, but for the majority a big part of their life is spent in school. It follows logically that much of the unacceptable behaviour displayed occurs in school. It is vitally important, therefore, to appreciate the levels of stress which can be imposed upon even the most supportive caring teacher. The context in which they work is a classroom, which is a fairly restricted space and does not lend itself easily to adaptation. Teachers are expected to deal with difficult behaviour displayed by troubled young people and at the same time provide effective support for all pupils in the class. In the average classroom, this can include between 20 and 30 young people. There is a tendency for some other professionals to reduce the complexities of the classroom situation because they have never actually experienced it. I am not trying in any way to minimise the input of other professional groups, but they must recognise that of all the professionals supporting young people, it is only the teacher who has to provide individual support in the rigid context of classrooms where everyone has the equal right to an education which fully develops their potential. Teachers have often to provide the additional support some young people need in this context with no extra help. Some professionals appeared not to see things in this way.

> Some teachers don't take a child-centred view. They just see the young person as troublesome and want to get rid of them. They say they have got to think of the needs of the others who don't misbehave, but in some ways I think this is a bit of a smokescreen.
> (Community Education Worker)

Having made this point, it is equally important for teachers to stand back now and then to try and extend their appreciation of the contexts in which other professionals operate. If they take the time to do so they will see that these professionals also face challenges relating to the role they perform when working in homes and in the community.

> Working with dysfunctional families can be really harrowing and it is difficult to distance yourself professionally and not be personally affected, although you know you must do so to do your job properly.
> (Social Worker)

> I get really amazed when teachers say that it must be great working in a one-to-one situation. It can be stressful working with an abused child and trying to help him express and come to terms with traumatic experiences.
> (Educational Psychologist)

It is inevitable that professionals will, to a large extent, continue to work in different contexts. This does not mean that they have to continue to misunderstand the nature of these contexts and the different challenges they present. Most professionals will be prepared to reflect upon some of the underlying issues and change their attitudes if they are given the opportunity. This puts the onus upon local authorities to start this process by developing continuing professional development opportunities which bring professionals together to explore these issues. As school is often the context which brings professionals together as a team, there is also an onus on schools to consider how they can become more conducive to collaborative inter-agency working.

Multidisciplinary partnerships

On the basis of the evidence gathered from the semi-structured interviews Hamill and Boyd (2000; 2003) concluded that the majority of professionals involved had internalised a child-centered approach. The majority appeared to appreciate that a holistic approach to meeting need was very important, but there appeared to be some confusion as to how their inputs might be best co-ordinated. Pickles (1994) helps clarify some of the concerns surrounding the preparation of staff to work in multidisciplinary teams when he says that this involves a proactive approach and involves considerable thought and planning:

> Most social workers, teachers and youth workers have been brought up almost entirely within their own traditions. These professional boundaries are well defined. They establish the unique cultures and ethos of each profession, its norms and working methods. They also carry a mythology about what people do. In this way professional identity can serve to defend the interests of one group and implicitly criticise another.
>
> (Pickles, 1994, p. 77)

If multi-agency approaches are to become a reality, then all professional efforts need to be fully integrated. Effective collaborative practice can only be put in place when the factors which encourage what Pickles refers to as the 'professional mythology' are challenged.

Language and communication

We must be wary of assuming that all professionals use language in the same way. They do not and this can pose problems in relation to what is said and what is actually received. This can be illustrated by considering certain words which can take on very different meanings depending on who is using them e.g. 'assessment', 'pupil', 'client', 'community', 'education', 'inclusion', 'need'. Language usage is underwritten by different professional value systems and assumptions based on these systems. The result can be stereotypical thinking which can create erroneous images that pose real barriers to inter-professional communication. There is a need for professionals to explore the essential differences in the way they use words or the myths will continue to thrive fed by a lack of information.

Co-ordinating services

I touched earlier on the fact that the common context which often brings professionals together is the school. This can be unfamiliar territory for some professionals who can find it difficult to fit into the more formal school systems. In such circumstances, confusion can occur in relation to professional roles and responsibilities, and these need to be clarified. This will necessitate the setting out of guidelines which show how the joined-up working practices and integrated working will operate. In addition, there is a need to appoint a key staff member who can assume responsibility for the co-ordination of all support services within the school context. This individual should also be responsible for evaluating and monitoring the quality of the service provided.

Continuing professional development

Different professional groups have unique specialist skills, knowledge and expertise, and care must be taken to ensure these are not diminished. The aim is to enhance the status of professionals by creating opportunities for them to cross professional boundaries, identify complementary skills and share expertise. Professionals have traditionally been locked within roles which have been too rigidly defined and there appears to be a need to blur the professional edges and help people see things from different perspectives rather than coming at things from a fairly restricted viewpoint. One way of blurring the professional boundaries and opening up channels of inter-professional communication is by bringing professionals together in inter-disciplinary forums. One professional made the case as follows:

> A lot of people clearly work with seriously disaffected young people or those on the social periphery. There is an urgent need for joint training but often the systems are not in place or set up in a way which can bring professionals together.
>
> (Social Worker)

This call for more joint inter-agency staff development is supported by other researchers (Rischly, 1988; Thomas, 1992; Jordan, 1994). However, the message is still not getting through to some local authorities who, while paying lip service to the theory underpinning more multidisciplinary working, are not necessarily doing all they can to make it a reality. I think it is reasonable to suggest that any local authority aiming to include disaffected young people in the mainstream school, raise their attainment and develop their potential, will find this very difficult if they do not address the issue of joined-up continuing professional development.

Moving forward

The studies undertaken by Hamill and Boyd (2000; 2003) provide evidence that multi-agency approaches are extremely important in relation to meeting effectively the additional support needs of young people who experience social, emotional and behavioral difficulties. It is now no longer acceptable for one group of professionals to operate in splendid isolation.

In 1995 the Children (Scotland) Act put the onus on local authorities to accept their corporate responsibility for the care and welfare of all young people. This meant that a duty was placed on all authorities to create forums where they could collaborate with and consult the full range of professional and voluntary agencies. This theme was taken up again in 1998 in the SOEID report entitled *Taking a Closer Look at Social Competence* (SOEID, 1998) which emphasised the view that a multi-agency strategy should be developed involving the full range of professionals who have a role to play supporting young people. The message conveyed is that there is much to be gained by combining forces to tackle problems and by pooling the full range of professional expertise. While it is true that over the past few years it has been acknowledged in principle that an increasing emphasis has been placed upon the benefits which can ensue when services operate holistically (Evans *et al.*, 1999; Dimmock, 2000; HMIE, 2002), in reality much practice remains unchanged.

There are few current educational initiatives which do not highlight the importance of collaborative inter-agency working. The theme is given prominence in the *Supporting Children's Learning: Code of Practice* (SE, 2005), particularly in relation to young people whose needs are complex and who require a co-ordinated support plan to ensure all relevant agencies are providing an integrated approach. This could include young people with social, emotional and behavioral needs.

How good is our school? The Journey to Excellence (HMIE, 2006) puts partnership with other agencies as one of the dimensions of excellence schools must strive to achieve, and the curriculum for excellence agenda emphasises the importance of inter-disciplinary working.

I would agree with Dryfoos (1995) who advocates the concept of the full-service school. She indicates that collaboration is a time-consuming business, and when the heat is on and professionals are stressed and under pressure, collaboration can be seen as a luxury. However, from their research Hamill and Boyd (2000; 2003) concluded that education and teachers alone cannot compensate for society. Bernstein argued this in 1970, and Mortimore and Whitty (1997) summed up the situation when they observed that it is totally unrealistic for schools to be expected to overcome issues relating to poverty, underachievement and challenging behavior, suggesting that the key to resolving some of these complex issues was inter-agency collaboration.

As we move further into the twenty-first century, it is absolutely essential that all professionals working with young people keep uppermost in their minds that everything they do is ultimately about empowering young people to be all they can be. At present, too many young people who display troubled and challenging behaviour become part of a game of pass the parcel. However, a young person is not a parcel to be passed between different professional groups. To treat someone as a problem to be passed from one agency to another belittles and trivialises the real issues the young person presents in school, in the community and at home. All professionals must think carefully about the pass-the-parcel mentality and create environments based upon openness and honesty where they can develop collaborative partnerships, and where the needs of young people are paramount.

SUMMARY

Young people whose behaviour can be challenging often come into contact with a range of professionals from various agencies. If the needs of these young people are to be addressed effectively it is vital that a holistic perspective is taken.

A systemic approach is important in relation to the assessment of behaviour and this involves consideration of the school, the home and the community. All of these contexts have an effect on behaviour and it is only by considering each of these interrelating systems that one can ascertain a truly comprehensive picture of a young person's behavioural needs.

It is not, however, always easy to bring professionals together and to date true inter-professional collaboration has to some extent eluded us.

It is, of course, true that there have always been real attempts made to rectify the situation and there are examples of good practice evident.

Over the past few years increasing numbers of education authorities have become more successful in relation to inter-agency working. In these authorities, care has been taken to identify openly and honestly potential barriers to inter-professional partnership and to try to resolve them. On the basis of Hamill and Boyd's research, some of these barriers have been identified and some suggestions for resolving them outlined. I have concluded that multidisciplinary partnerships must become a reality, particularly for those whose additional support needs result from their social, emotional and behavioural difficulties. For these young people this professional co-operation is not optional. It is critical.

POINTS FOR REFLECTION

1 To support effectively young people whose behaviour is disruptive, it is important that all professionals work in partnership, and that the services they provide are integrated. Based on your own personal and professional experience, to what extent is this situation evident?

2 When inter-agency forums are set up to promote joined-up working, are all professional contributions equally valued?

3 What are the barriers which hinder professional collaboration and how might they be overcome so that young people's needs can be addressed holistically?

References

Chapter 1

Ainscow, M. (1991) *Effective Schools for All* London: David Fulton

Barber, M. (1996) *The Learning Game* London: Indigo

Becker, H.S. (1963) *Outsiders* New York: Free Press

Booth, T. and Coulby, D. (Eds) (1987) *Producing and Reducing Disaffection* Milton Keynes: Open University Press

Cole, T., Visser, J. and Upton, G. (1998) *Effective Schooling for Pupils with Emotional and Behavioural Difficulties* London: David Fulton

Cooper, P. (1993) *Effective Schools for Disaffected Students: Integration and Segregation* London: Routledge

DES (Department of Education and Science) (1978) *Special Educational Needs. Report of the Committee of Enquiry into the Education of Handicapped Children and Young People (The Warnock Report)* London: HMSO

DES (1993*) Education for Disaffected Pupils* London: HMSO

Education (Additional Support for Learning) (Scotland) Act 2004

Education Act 1944

Evans, J., Lunt, I., Weddell, K. and Dyson, A. (1999) *Collaborating for Effectiveness: Empowering Schools to be Inclusive* Buckingham: Open University Press

Farrell, P. (1995) *Children with Emotional and Behavioural Difficulties: Strategies for Assessment and Intervention* London: Falmer Press

Fogell, J. and Long, R. (1997) *Spotlight on Special Educational Needs – Emotional and Behavioural Difficulties* Staffs: NASEN

Ford, J., Mongon, D., and Whelan, M. (1982) *Special Education and Social Control* London: Routledge

Furlong, V.J. (1985) *The Deviant Pupil Sociological Perspectives* Milton Keynes: Open University Press

Galloway, D.M., Armstrong, D. and Tomlinson, S. (1994) *The Assessment of Special Educational Needs: Whose Problem?* Harlow: Longman

Garner, P. and Gains, C. (1996) 'Models of Intervention for Children with Emotional and Behavioural Difficulties' *Support for Learning* 11(4) 141–5

Gilbert, C. and Hart, M. (1990) *Towards Integration* London: Kogan Page

Hamill, P. and Boyd, B. (2000) *Striving for Inclusion* Glasgow: University of Strathclyde

Hamill, P. and Boyd, B. (2003) *Inclusion: Principles into Practice* Glasgow: University of Strathclyde

The Handicapped Pupils and School Health Regulations 1945

Herbert, M. (1993) *Working with Children and the Children Act* London: BPS

HMIE (HM Inspectorate of Education) (2002) *Count Us In – Achieving Inclusion in Scottish Schools* Edinburgh: HMIE

Laslett, R. (1983) *Changing Perceptions of Maladjusted Children (1945–1981)* Portishead: AWMC

Laurie, A.P. (Ed) (1912) *The Teachers' Encyclopaedia* Vol V London: Caxton Ltd

Mental Deficiency Act 1913

MoE (Ministry of Education) (1955) *Underwood Report of the Committee on Maladjusted Children* London: HMSO

Montgomery, D. (1998) *Managing Behaviour Problems* London: Hodder and Stoughton

O'Brien, T. (1998) *Promoting Positive Behaviour* London: David Fulton

Porter, L. (2007) *Behaviour in Schools – Theory and Practice for Teachers* Buckingham: Open University Press

Reid, J. (1987) 'A Problem in the Family: Explanations Under Strain' in Booth, T. and Coulby, D. (Eds) *Producing and Reducing Disaffection* Milton Keynes: Open University Press

Reynolds, D. and Sullivan, M. (1981) 'The Effects of School: A Radical Faith' in Gillham, B. (Ed.) *Problem Behaviour in the Secondary School* London: Croom Helm

Rutter, M., Maugham, B., Mortimore, P. and Ouston, J. (1979) *Fifteen Thousand Hours: Secondary Schools and their Effect on Children* London: Open Books

SCCC (Scottish Consultative Council on the Curriculum) (1993) *Support for Learning: Special Educational Needs Within the 5–14 Curriculum* Edinburgh: HMSO

SCF (Scottish Council Foundation) (1999) *Children, Families and Learning – A New Agenda for Education* Edinburgh: SCF

SE (Scottish Executive) (2005) *Supporting Children's Learning: Code of Practice* Edinburgh: Astron

SEED (Scottish Executive Education Department) (2003) *Moving Forward! Additional Support for Learning* Edinburgh: HMSO

SOED (Scottish Office Education Department) (1994) *Effective Provision for Special Educational Needs* Edinburgh: HMSO

SOEID (Scottish Office Education and Industry Department) (1999) *A Manual of Good Practice in Special Educational Needs* Edinburgh: HMSO

Special Educational Treatment (Scotland) Regulations 1954

Standards in Scotland's Schools Etc. Act 2000

Ullman, L. and Krasner, K. (1965) *Case Studies in Behaviour Modification* London: Holt Rinehart and Winston

Chapter 2

Ayers, H., Clarke, D. and Murray, A. (1995) *Perspectives on Behaviour – A Practical Guide to Effective Interventions for Teachers* London: David Fulton

Bandura, A. (1977) *Social Learning Theory* Englewood Cliffs NJ: Prentice Hall

Bowlby, J. (1971) *Attachment and Loss Vols 1–3* Harmondsworth: Penguin

Bronfenbrenner, U. (1979) *The Ecology of Human Development* Cambridge MA: Harvard University Press

Cole, T., Visser, J. and Upton, G. (1998) *Effective Schooling for Pupils with Emotional and Behavioural Difficulties* London: David Fulton

Cooper, P. (2004) 'Nurture Groups: The Research Evidence' in Wearmouth, J., Richmond, R.C. and Glynn, T. (Eds) *Addressing Pupils' Behaviour Response at District School and Individual Levels* London: David Fulton

Dowling, E. and Osborne, E. (Eds) (1994) *The Family and the School* (2nd edn) London: Routledge

Farrell, P. (1995) *Children with Emotional and Behavioural Difficulties: Strategies for Assessment and Intervention* London: Falmer Press

Farrell, M. (2006) *Behavioural, Emotional and Social Difficulties – Practical Strategies* Oxon: Routledge

Glenn, A., Cousins, J. and Helps, A. (2004) *Behaviour in the Early Years* London: David Fulton

Laslett, R. (1977) 'Disruptive Pupils the Fact and the Fallacies' Education Review 29(3) 152–62

Leaman, L. (2005) *Managing Very Challenging Behaviour* London: Continuum

McSherry, J. (2001) *Challenging Behaviours in Mainstream Schools: Practical Strategies for Intervention and Reintegration* London: David Fulton

Mischel, W. (1973) 'Towards a Cognitive Social Learning – Reconceptualisation of the Personality' *Psychological Review* Vol 80

Molnar, A. and Lindquist, B. (1989) *Changing Problem Behaviour in Schools* San Francisco: Jossey-Bass

Porter, L. (2007) *Behaviour in Schools – Theory and Practice for Teachers* (2nd edn) Buckingham: Open University Press

Rogers, B. (Ed.) (2004) *How to Manage Children's Behaviour* London: Paul Chapman

SEED (Scottish Executive Education Department) (2001) *Better Behaviour – Better Learning Report of Discipline Task Group* Edinburgh: HMSO

Winnicott, D. (1991) *The Child, the Family and the Outside World* Harmondsworth: Penguin

Chapter 3

Ayers, H., Clarke, D. and Ross, A. (2006) *Assessing Individual Needs – A Practical Approach* (2nd edn) London: David Fulton

Bridgeland, M. (1971) *Pioneer Work with Maladjusted Children* London: Staples

Cole, T., Visser, J. and Upton, G. (1998) *Effective Schooling for Pupils with Emotional and Behavioural Difficulties* London: David Fulton

Davie, R. (1993) 'Assessing and Understanding Children's Behaviour' in Charlton, T. and David, K. *Managing Misbehaviour in Schools* London: Routledge

Education (Additional Support for Learning) (Scotland) 2004 Act

Fawcett, M. (1996) *Learning Through Child Observation* London: Jessica Kingsley

Furlong, V.J. (1985) *The Deviant Pupil Sociological Perspectives* Milton Keynes: Open University Press

Hamill, P. and Boyd, B. (2000) *Striving for Inclusion* Glasgow: University of Strathclyde

Hamill, P. and Boyd, B. (2003) *Inclusion: Principles into Practice* Glasgow: University of Strathclyde

The Handicapped Pupils and School Health Regulations 1945

Hargreaves, D.H., Astor, S.K. and Mellor, F.J. (1975) *Deviance in the Classroom* London: Routledge and Kegan Paul

Hill, F. and Parsons, L. (2000) *Teamwork in the Management of Emotional and Behavioural Difficulties* London: David Fulton

Hull Learning Services (2005) *Supporting Children with Behavioural Difficulties* London: David Fulton

Laslett, R. (1983) *Changing Perceptions of Maladjusted Children (1945–1981)* Portishead: AWMC

Laurie, A.P. (Ed.) (1912) *The Teachers' Encyclopaedia* Vol V London: Caxton Ltd

Lloyd, G. and Munn, P. (1999) 'Educational Services for Children with Social, Emotional or Behavioural Difficulties' in Hill, M. *Effective Ways of Working with Children and their Families* London: Jessica Kingsley

Mehan, H. (1996) 'The Politics of Representation' in Chaiklin, S. and Lave, J. (Eds) *Understanding Practice: Perspectives on Activity and Context* Cambridge: Cambridge University Press

Mental Deficiency Act 1913

MoE (Ministry of Education) (1955) *Underwood Report of the Committee on Maladjusted Children* London: HMSO

Nisbet, J.D. (1977) 'Small Scale Research Guidelines and Suggestions for Development' *Scottish Educational Studies* 9 May: 13–17

Rutter, M. (1967) 'A Children's Behaviour Questionnaire for Completion by Teachers' *Journal of Psychology and Psychiatry* 8: 1–11

Rutter, M., Maugham, B., Mortimore, P. and Ouston, J. (1979) *Fifteen Thousand Hours: Secondary Schools and their Effect on Children* London: Open Books

SE (Scottish Executive) (2005) *Supporting Children's Learning: Code of Practice* Edinburgh: Astron

SEED (Scottish Executive Education Department) (2001) *Better Behaviour – Better Learning Report of the Discipline Task Group* Edinburgh: HMSO

Sharma, C., Cross, W. and Vennis, D. (2000) *A Practical Guide – Observing Children* (3rd edn) London: Continuum

Simpson, M. and Tuson, J. (2003) *Using Observations in Small Scale research* Glasgow: University of Glasgow

SOEID (Scottish Office Education and Industry Department) (1998) *Guidance on Issues Concerning Exclusion from School* Circular 2/98 Edinburgh: HMSO

Stott, D.H. (1974) *The Bristol Social Adjustment Guides* London: Hodder and Stoughton

Tizard, J. (1973) 'The Problem Child in Schools' *London Educational Review* 12(2) Summer 1973

UN (United Nations) (1990) Convention on the Rights of the Child Article 12

Wearmouth, J. and Cole, T. (2004) 'Issues in Inclusion and the Management of Student Behaviour in Schools' in Wearmouth, J. *et al.* (Eds) *Inclusion and Behaviour Management in Schools: Issues and Challenges* London: David Fulton

Chapter 4

Ainscow, M. (1999) *Understanding the Development of the Inclusive School* London: Falmer Press

Bailey, J. (1998) 'Australia: Inclusion through Categorization' in Booth, T. and Ainscow, M. (Eds) *From them to Us – An International Study of Inclusion in Education* London Routledge

Barber, M. (1996) *The Learning Game* London: Indigo

Barton, L. (1997) 'Inclusive Education: Romantic Subversive or Realistic?' *International Journal of Inclusive Education* 1(3) 231–42

Booth, T. and Ainscow, M. (1998) *From them to Us – An International Study of Inclusion in Education* London: Routledge

Cigman, R. (2007) *Included or Excluded – The Challenge of the Mainstream for some SEN Children* Oxon: Routledge

Cooper, P. (1993) *Effective Schools for Disaffected Students: Integration and Segregation* London: Routledge

CSIE (Centre for Studies in Inclusive Education) New Redlands, Frenchay Campus, Coldharbour Lane, Bristol (www.csie.org.uk)

(2007) A Curriculum for Excellence www.acurriculumforexcellencescotland.gov.uk

Dyson, A. (1997) 'Social and Educational Disadvantage: Reconnecting Special Needs Education' *British Journal of Special Education* 24(4)152–7

Education Act 1993

Farrell, M. (2004) *Inclusion at the Crossroad: Special Education Concepts and Values* London: David Fulton

Hamill, P. and Boyd, B. (2000) *Striving for Inclusion* Glasgow: University of Strathclyde

Hamill, P. and Boyd, B. (2003) *Inclusion: Principles into Practice* Glasgow: University of Strathclyde

HMIE (HM Inspectorate of Education) (2002) *Count Us In – Achieving Inclusion in Scottish Schools* Edinburgh: HMIE (www.hmie.gov.uk)

Low, C. (1997) 'Is Inclusiveism Possible?' *European Journal of Special Needs Education* 12(1) 71–9

Mittler, P. (2000) *Working Towards Inclusive Education: Social Contexts* London: David Fulton

Nind, M., Sheehy, K. and Simmons, K. (2003) *Inclusive Education Learners and Learning Contexts* London: David Fulton

O'Brien, T. (1998) *Promoting Positive Behaviour* London: David Fulton

O'Brien, T. (Ed.) (2001) *Enabling Inclusion Blue Skies – Dark Clouds?* London: The Stationery Office

Porter, L. (2007) *Behaviour in Schools – Theory and Practice for Teachers* (2nd edn) Milton Keynes: Open University Press

Rustemier, S. (2002) *Social and Educational Justice – The Human Rights Framework for Inclusion* Bristol: CSIE

SE (Scottish Executive) (2005) *Supporting Children's Learning: Code of Practice* Edinburgh: Astron

SOED (Scottish Office Education Department) (1988) *Effective Secondary Schools* Edinburgh: HMSO

SOED (1989) *Effective Primary Schools* Edinburgh: HMSO

SOED (1994) *5–14 A Practical Guide* Edinburgh: HMSO

SOEID (Scottish Office Education and Industry Department) (1996) *Achievement for All* Edinburgh: HMSO

Standards in Scotland's Schools Act Etc. 2000

Thomas, G., Walker, D. and Webb, J. (1998) *The Making of the Inclusive School* London: Routledge

Topping, K. and Maloney, S. (Eds) (2005) *Inclusive Education* London: Routledge

UN (United Nations) (1990) Convention on the Rights of the Child Article 12

UNESCO (1994) *Salamanca Statement and Framework for Action on Special Educational Needs* Paris: UNESCO

Warnock, M. (2005) *Special Educational Needs: A New Look* London: Philosophy of Education Society of Great Britain www.nationalpriorities.org.uk

Chapter 5

(2007) A Curriculum for Excellence www.acurriculum forexcellencescotland.gov.uk

Bantock, G.H. (1980) *Dilemmas of the Curriculum* London: Methuen

Booth, T. and Coulby, D. (Eds) (1987) *Producing and Reducing Disaffection* Milton Keynes: Open University Press

Cole, T., Visser, J. and Upton, G. (1998) *Effective Schooling for Pupils with Emotional and Behavioural Difficulties* London: David Fulton

Coulby, D. (1987) 'Changing Urban Schools' in Booth, T. and Coulby, D. (Eds) *Producing and Reducing Disaffection* Milton Keynes: Open University Press

Farrell, P. (1995) *Children with Emotional and Behavioural Difficulties: Strategies for Assessment and Intervention* London: Falmer Press

Garner, P. and Gains, C. (1996) 'Models of Intervention for Children with Emotional and Behavioural Difficulties' *Support for Learning* 11(4) 141–5

Glasser, W. (1998) *The Quality School: Managing Students Without Coercion* New York: Harper Perennial

Hamill, P. and Boyd, B. (2000) *Striving for Inclusion* Glasgow: University of Strathclyde

Hamill, P. and Boyd, B. (2003) *Inclusion: Principles into Practice* Glasgow: University of Strathclyde

HMIE (HM Inspectorate of Education) (2002) *Count Us In – Achieving Inclusion in Scottish Schools* Edinburgh: HMIE www.hmie.gov.uk

Kelly, A.V. (2004) *The Curriculum – Theory and Practice* (5th edn) London: Sage

O'Brien, T. (1998) *Promoting Positive Behaviour* London: David Fulton

Olsen, J. and Cooper, P. (2001) *Dealing with Disruptive Students in the Classroom* London: Kogan Page

Richmond, K. (1971) *The School Curriculum* London: Methuen

SCCC (Scottish Consultative Committee on the Curriculum) (1986) *10–14 Report*

SED (Scottish Education Department) (1978) *The Education of Pupils with Learning Difficulties in Primary and Secondary Schools in Scotland* Edinburgh: HMSO

SEED (Scottish Executive Education Department) (2001) *Better Behaviour – Better Learning Report of the Discipline Task Group* Edinburgh: HMSO

Smith, C.J. (1992) 'Management of Special Needs' in Gulliford, R. and Upton, G. (Eds) *Special Educational Needs* London: Routledge

Solity, J. (1993) *Special Education* London: Cassell

Woods, P. and Orlik, A. (1994) *School Review and Inspection* London: Kogan Paul

Chapter 6

Carlock, C.J. (1998) *Enhancing Self-esteem* (3rd edn) Philadelphia: Taylor and Francis Group

Freiberg, H.J. and Stein, T.A. (1999) 'Three Creative Ways to Measure School Climate and Next Steps' in Freiberg, H.J. (Ed.) *School Climate: Measuring Improving and Sustaining Healthy Learning Environments* London: Falmer Press

Hamill, P. and Boyd, B. (2000) *Striving for Inclusion* Glasgow: University of Strathclyde

Hamill, P. and Boyd, B. (2003) *Inclusion: Principles into Practice* Glasgow: University of Strathclyde

Hamill, P. and Clark, K. (2005) *Additional Support Needs – An Introduction to ASN from Nursery to Secondary* Paisley: Hodder Gibson

Harlen, W. and Malcolm, H. (1997) *Setting and Streaming* Edinburgh: SCRE

Kyriacou, C. (1998) *Effective Teaching in Schools* (2nd edn) Cheltenham: Nelson Thornes

Lawrence, D. (1996) *Enhancing Self-esteem in the Classroom* (2nd edn) London: Paul Chapman

Leaman, L. (2005) *Managing Very Challenging Behaviour* London: Continuum

McLean, A. (1991) *Promoting Positive Behaviour in the Primary School* Glasgow: Strathclyde Regional Council

McNamara, S. and Moreton, G. (2001) *Changing Behaviour – Teaching Children with Emotional and Behavioural Difficulties in Primary and Secondary Classrooms* (2nd edn) London: David Fulton

Muijs, D. and Reynolds, D. (2001) *Effective Teaching – Evidence and Practice* London: Paul Chapman

Rogers, B. (2004) *Behaviour Recovery* (2nd edn) London: Paul Chapman

Rosenthal, R. and Jacobsen, L. (1968) *Pygmalion in the Classroom* New York: Holt Rinehart and Wilson

Rutter, M., Maugham, B., Mortimore, P. and Ouston, J. (1979) *Fifteen Thousand Hours: Secondary Schools and their Effect on Children* London: Open Books

SEED (Scottish Executive Education Department) (2001) *Better Behaviour – Better Learning Report of the Discipline Task Group* Edinburgh: HMSO

Stradling, B. and Saunders, L. (1993) 'Differentiation in Practice; Responding to the Needs of all Pupils' *Educational Research* 135: 127–37

Chapter 7

Ainscow, M. (1991) *Effective Schools for All* London: David Fulton

Bolam, R. (1999) 'Educational Administration, Leadership and Management: Towards a Research Agenda' in Bush, T., Bell, L., Bolam, R., Glatter, R. and Ribbins, P. (Eds) *Educational Management: Redefining Theory, Policy and Practice* London: Paul Chapman

Bush, T. and Middlewood, D. (2005) *Leading and Managing People in Education* London: Sage

Emmett, S. (2004) *The Discipline Pocketbook* Hampshire: Management Pocketbooks

Harris, A. (2002) 'Effective Leadership in Schools: Facing the Challenge' in *School Leadership and Management* 22(1) 15–26

Hook, P. and Vass, A. (2004) *Behaviour Management Pocketbook* Hampshire: Teachers' Pocketbooks

Leaman, L. (2005) *Managing Very Challenging Behaviour* London: Continuum

MacBeath, J. and Mortimore, P. (Eds) (2001) *Improving School Effectiveness* Buckingham: Open University Press

McBer, H. (2000) *Research into Teacher Effectiveness – A Model of Teacher Effectiveness* London: Department for Education and Employment

Mortimore, P., Sammons, P., Stoll, L., Lewis, D. and Ecob, R. (1988) *School Matters: The Junior Years* Somerset: Open Books (reprinted 1994 London: Paul Chapman)

Olsen, J. and Cooper, P. (2001) *Dealing with Disruptive Students in the Classroom* London: Kogan Page

Rogers, B. (2000) *Behaviour Management: A Whole School Approach* London: Paul Chapman

Rogers, B. (2004) *Behaviour Recovery* (2nd edn) London: Paul Chapman

Rutter, M., Maugham, B., Mortimore, P. and Ouston, J. (1979) *Fifteen Thousand Hours: Secondary Schools and their Effect on Children* London: Open Books

Scheerens, J. (1997) 'Theories on Effective Schooling' in *School Effectiveness and School Improvement* 8(3) 220–42

williamarthurward.com/

Chapter 8

Armstrong, D. (1995) *Power and Partnership: Parents, Children and Special Educational Needs* London: Routledge

DES (Department of Education and Science) (1967) *Children and their Primary Schools: Report of the Central Advisory Council for Education (Plowden Report)* London: HMSO

Dowling, M. (2005) *Young Children's Personal, Social and Emotional Development* London: Paul Chapman

Hamill, P. and Boyd, B. (2000) *Striving for Inclusion* Glasgow: University of Strathclyde

Hamill, P. and Boyd, B. (2003) *Inclusion: Principles into Practice* Glasgow: University of Strathclyde

HMIE (HM Inspectorate of Education) (2006) *How good is our school? The Journey to Excellence* Edinburgh: HMIE www.hmie.gov.uk

Katz, L. (1995) *Talks with Teachers of Young Children* Norwood NJ: Ablex

McIntyre, D. and Cooper, P. (1996) *Effective Teaching and Learning: Teachers' and Pupils' Perspectives* Buckingham: Open University Press

Mittler, P. and Mittler, H. (Eds) (1994) *Innovation in Family Support* Chorley: Lisieux Hall Press

Rogers, C.R. (1980) *A Way of Being* Boston: Houghton Mills

Scottish Council Foundation (1999) *Children, Families and Learning* Edinburgh: SCF

Strauss, A. and Corbin, J. (1990) *Qualitative Analysis for Social Scientists* Cambridge: Cambridge University Press

Wolfendale, S. (1992) *Empowering Parents and Teachers* London: Cassell

Chapter 9

Cole, T., Visser, J. and Upton, G. (1998) *Effective Schooling for Pupils with Emotional and Behavioural Difficulties* London: David Fulton

Cooper, P., Drummond, M., Hart, S., Lovey, J. and McLaughlin, C. (2000) *Positive Alternatives to Exclusion* London: Routledge

Cullingford, C. (1999) *The Causes of Exclusion* London: Kogan Page

Davies, J.D. (2005) 'Voices from the Margins: The Perceptions of Pupils with Emotional and Behavioural Difficulties about their Educational Experience' in Garner, P. *et al.* (Eds) *Handbook of Emotional and Behavioural Difficulties* London: Sage

Education (Additional Support for Learning) (Scotland) Act 2004

Garner, P. (1999) 'Schools by Scoundrels – The views of disruptive pupils in mainstream schools in England and the United States' in Lloyd-Smith, M. and David, J.D. (Eds) *On the Margins – the Educational Experience of Problem Pupils* Stoke-on-Trent: Trentham Books

Hamill, P. and Boyd, B. (2000) *Striving for Inclusion* Glasgow: University of Strathclyde

Hamill, P. and Boyd, B. (2003) *Inclusion: Principles into Practice* Glasgow: University of Strathclyde

Montgomery, D. (1998) *Reversing Lower Attainment – Developmental Curriculum Strategies for Overcoming Disaffection and Underachievement* London: David Fulton

Nieto, S. (1994) 'Lessons from Students on Creating a Chance to Dream' *Harvard Educational Review* 64(4) 392–426

Olsen, J. and Cooper, P. (2001) *Dealing with Disruptive Students in the Classroom* London: Kogan Page

Pomeroy, E. (2000) *Experiencing Exclusion* Stoke on Trent: Trentham Books

Porter, L. (2007) *Behaviour in Schools – Theory and Practice for Teachers* (2nd edn) Buckingham: Open University Press

Rutter, M., Maugham, B., Mortimore, P. and Ouston, J. (1979) *Fifteen Thousand Hours: Secondary Schools and their Effect on Children* London: Open Books

SE (Scottish Executive) (2005) *Supporting Children's Learning: Code of Practice* Edinburgh: Astron

Standards in Scotland's Schools Etc. Act 2000

Tattum, D. (1982) *Disruptive Pupils in Schools and Units* London: Wiley and Sons

The Education (Additional Support for Learning) (Scotland) Act 2004

Thomas, G. and Loxley, A. (2004) 'The great problem of 'need': a case study into children who don't behave' in Wearmouth, J. et al. (Eds) *Inclusion and Behaviour Management in Schools: Issues and Challenges* London: David Fulton

Thomas, G., Walker, D. and Webb, J. (1998) *The Making of the Inclusive School* London: Routledge

UN (United Nations) (1990) *Convention on the Rights of the Child* Articles 12 and 23

Chapter 10

Bernstein, B. (1970) 'Education Cannot Compensate for Society' *New Society* 15: 344–7

Children (Scotland) Act 1995

Cooper, P., Drummond, M.J., Hart, S., Lovey, J. and McLaughlin, C. (2000) *Positive Alternatives to Exclusion* London: Routledge Falmer

Dimmock, C. (2000) *Designing the Learning Centred School* London: Falmer

Dryfoos, J.G. (1995) 'Full Service Schools Revolution or Fad?' *Journal of Research on Adolescence* 5(2) 147–72

Evans, J., Lunt, I., Weddell, K. and Dyson, A. (1999) *Collaborating for Effectiveness: Empowering Schools to be Inclusive* Buckingham: Open University Press

Hamill, P. and Boyd, B. (2000) *Striving for Inclusion* Glasgow: University of Strathclyde

Hamill, P. and Boyd, B. (2003) *Inclusion: Principles into Practice* Glasgow: University of Strathclyde

HMIE (HM Inspectorate of Education) (2002) *Count Us In – Achieving Inclusion in Scottish Schools* Edinburgh: HMIE www.hmie.gov.uk

HMIE (2006) *How good is our school? The Journey to Excellence* Edinburgh: HMIE www.hmie.gov.uk

Jordan, A. (1994) *Skills in Collaborative Classroom Consultation* London: Routledge

Mittler, P. (2000) *Working Towards Inclusive Education: Social Contexts* London: David Fulton

Mortimore, P. and Whitty, G. (1997) *Can School Improvement Overcome the Effects of Disadvantage?* London: University of London Institute of Education

Pickles, T. (1994) *Teachers and Social Workers – Working Together in Challenging Behaviour in Schools* London: Routledge

Rischly, D.J. (1988) *Special Education Reform School Psychology Revolution* London: Open Books

SE (Scottish Executive) (2005) *Supporting Children's Learning: Code of Practice* Edinburgh: HMSO

SEED (Scottish Office Education Department) (2001) *Better Behaviour – Better Learning Report of Discipline Task Group* Edinburgh: HMSO

SO (The Scottish Office) (1999) *New Community Schools – The Prospectus* Edinburgh: HMSO

SOEID (Scottish Office Education and Industry Department) (1998) *Taking a Closer Look at Promoting Social Competence* Edinburgh: HMSO

Thomas, G. (1992) *Effective Classroom Teamwork: Support or Intrusion?* London: Routledge

Index